TWELVE NEGRO AMERICANS

TWELVE
NEGRO
AMERICANS

BY MARY JENNESS

Essay Index Reprint Series

BOOKS FOR LIBRARIES PRESS
FREEPORT, NEW YORK

First Published 1936
Reprinted 1969

STANDARD BOOK NUMBER:
8369-1143-1

LIBRARY OF CONGRESS CATALOG CARD NUMBER:
74-86764

PRINTED IN THE UNITED STATES OF AMERICA

CONTENTS

v

CONTENTS

FOREWORD

THE NEGRO AMERICANS whose work is described in
this collection of sketches have been chosen for the
sake of the varied fields of service which they represent as much as for their personalities. Here, for
example, is the area of cooperative business, represented by the manager of one of the two most successful Negro cooperatives in the United States.
Other fields included are those of education, student
work, social work, rural improvement, and the city
church. Some of the Negroes written about are at
work among Negroes, and some of them are working
among Americans of all races.

The fields of art, music and literature have been
left out for several reasons. First, Negro achievement in these fields is widely known and is the subject of many recent books. But the Negro's contribution in many other fields has been less fully described.

Most Negroes, like most whites, are not in the
spotlight, but an increasing number of them are
trained people who are quietly doing a good job that

never gets into the headlines. For example, the Jeanes supervisor of rural schools whose story is told here has not become known outside her state, nor the social worker outside her city. Yet such stories as these should be better known to young people, both colored and white, because in them the whole Negro race may be seen coming forward.

Anyone familiar with Negro leadership in America today will think instantly of many Negroes whose stories are as interesting and inspiring as any in this book. The author has selected those individuals whose work represented the desired range of service and whose achievements were known to her or to Negro and white friends in a position to furnish sufficiently detailed information.

Once the list of names was determined, Negro men and women practically wrote this book about their friends. The Negro contributors include a pleasant variety of neighbors and associates, among them a retired mail carrier, deacons old and young, home mission school teachers, college classmates, and Y.M.C.A. and Y.W.C.A. secretaries. In one case a special source became available when a college official induced the Jeanes teacher to dictate a five-thousand-word autobiography on the ground of the importance of the little known kind of rural work which she is doing.

It is to Miss Marion Cuthbert that the author is especially indebted for counsel and suggestion in planning the book and securing material. Hers is a name to be trusted and when the plea was sent, "Marion Cuthbert says that you will be glad to tell what you know about this friend of yours," letters came back quickly from friendly people in many states. Miss Cuthbert was formerly the dean of Talladega College in Talladega, Alabama, and is a familiar figure in student conferences through the South. Later she came to New York City on a Kent scholarship, and secured her Ph.D. at Columbia University. Now she is in the Leadership Division of the National Board of the Y.W.C.A., in which capacity she travels all over the country. She is therefore more widely known than some of the people in the book, but she refused to be included, preferring to help behind the scenes as sponsor and adviser.

Special information has been freely given by the National Association for the Advancement of Colored People; the National Urban League; the National Negro Rural School Fund, Inc.; the Phelps-Stokes Fund; the Department of Race Relations of the Fed-

eral Council of Churches; the Commission on Inter-
racial Cooperation; the National Council of Student
Christian Associations; Dr. Channing H. Tobias,
Senior Secretary for Colored Work of the Y.M.C.A.;
and by Dr. Ambrose Caliver, Senior Specialist in the
Education of Negroes, U. S. Office of Education.

Many church organizations have also given assistance; among these are the American Missionary Association; the Woman's American Baptist Home Mission Society; the Board of American Missions of the
United Presbyterian Church of North America; and
the Woman's Auxiliary to the National Council of
the Protestant Episcopal Church.

MARY JENNESS

New York City
May, 1936

TWELVE NEGRO AMERICANS

ONE

BETTER FARMS FOR BETTER FARMERS

WHEN Thomas Monroe Campbell took the entrance examinations at Tuskegee Institute, his rating was so low that he did not make any grade at all. He was classified below the lowest grade in the school, but he was given the chance to enter as a "work student" and make a grade through the evening classes as soon as he could. "For a while," he says, "I worked all day and studied all night." The fact was that this sixteen-year-old boy had been able to get less than a full year of schooling in all his life—an average of less than a month a year. He explains why in a recent book about his present job, *The Movable School Goes to the Negro Farmer*.[1]

"Those of us who happen to have been born on Southern plantations," he writes, "have vivid memories of hearing the landlord announce to our parents about the middle of January each year that owing to the fact that it was time to begin 'strewing guano'

[1] Tuskegee Press, Tuskegee Institute, Alabama, 1936. By permission.

and scattering manure over the cotton land, they would have to take their children out of school. . . . After the land was prepared, the crop planted, worked and 'laid by' in July, our hearts would be made glad as we were sent forth once more with our books and dinner pails to the little school down on the creek. All went well with us to the middle of August, when notice came from the landlord that because the cotton was opening, it was necessary for all hands to turn to gathering the fleecy staple. The result now is as it was then: thousands of rural Negro children growing into manhood and womanhood dangerously and pitifully ignorant."

However, thanks to Thomas Campbell himself, the results of the sharecropping system are not quite so bad for colored boys and girls as they were when he was a boy. He not only worked his own way up out of a desperate situation, but since he grew up he has been showing that way to farmers of the seven Gulf states. Until he was twelve years old, though, no road to anything but endless cotton-picking and hard farm work ever opened ahead of him. That was his age when he first heard of Booker T. Washington. Till then one season had been like another, except that life grew harder and poorer all the time as more children came into that Methodist preacher's family.

Thomas Campbell was the second son. He was born the day before Lincoln's birthday in 1883, just outside the town of Bowman, Georgia. The father moved from one rented farm to another, never making any headway on the worn-out soil. In those days poor soil stayed poor because no one, least of all a colored farmer, knew how to feed it. He was lucky if he could feed his own children. The only cash that ever came in was earned by picking cotton on some white man's plantation or by hiring out the children to pick it in what should have been school time.

The whole South was still so poor that it could hardly provide schools for any children, colored or white. At the end of the Civil War thirty years before, both races had started practically empty-handed, as Booker T. Washington used to say. Ever since then both had been bound in a chain of misfortune: exhausted soil meant poor crops, poor crops meant little money, and lack of money meant poor schools or none. Elbert County did well in providing several three-month schools for Negroes, but Thomas could attend for only about one month each year. What more could he expect, when his sisters were working in the fields like men?

In 1895, when Thomas was twelve years old, people all around him burst into excited reports of Booker T. Washington's speech at the Cotton States Exposition in Atlanta, Georgia. That famous speech is printed in full in *Up from Slavery*, but to measure the full force of it one has to watch the effect on the two Campbell boys. The next term the older one took all the money that he had been able to save from his cotton picking and started off for Tuskegee Institute. Thomas promptly asked his father to start saving money for him so that he might follow his brother. Somehow the money never could be saved, and three years later Thomas Campbell decided that he must do something now or never, and he must do it alone. He ran away from home and started, penniless, down one of the orange clay roads toward Tuskegee Institute, two hundred and thirty miles away. It took him three months to get there because he was not a hitch-hiker. He was a work-hiker.

It was the last of April in 1898 before he reached Tuskegee Institute and his first hero, Booker T. Washington. Tuskegee Institute had been founded eighteen years previously, and forty-odd buildings had been built by student labor to house the eleven hundred boys and girls and the farm equipment. This was just before the time when Booker T. Washington applied to Andrew Carnegie for a library on the basis that all of the brick work, masonry and carpentry would be done by the students. Mr. Washington was now too busy raising money for the school to do any teaching himself at Tuskegee, but his spirit filled the place.

This is Mr. Campbell's own report of that first examination at Tuskegee Institute, already noted: "My training was such that I was unable to make the lowest class, and I sometimes think that my only salvation was that I was large and strong and my services were needed on the farm. By constant study, both day and night, I was able to make a class the next year and every year until my graduation in 1906."

In other words, this boy, like many at that time and some nowadays, was admitted as a "work student," that is, one who works to support himself as he studies to make his place in the graded system. Three months after Thomas's arrival at Tuskegee his older brother suddenly died, and the boy found himself entirely on his own. His father managed to send him two dollars in cash and one suit of clothes

7

during his eight years at Tuskegee. Thomas went on working his way as carriage boy, farm tool boy, and milker of farm cows. During vacations he followed public works, doing whatever a tall and husky boy could do. He went out logging, railroad grading, and once he was a teamster for the U. S. Geological Survey—his first government job.

Soon after Thomas Campbell made his class at Tuskegee his story became linked with that of George Washington Carver. Professor Carver is now internationally known as the research chemist who has been able to make nearly two hundred by-products from the peanut and a hundred out of the sweet potato. He has been listed in *Who's Who in America* since 1930. In those days he was making his job as he went along. He had come to the campus just five years before from Iowa State College, and he had started his first students searching in rubbish heaps for the empty bottles and bits of rubber and wire with which his now famous laboratory began. He refers to Mr. Campbell with pride as "one of my first boys."

After eight years Thomas Campbell had completed all of Professor Carver's courses and everything else that the high school of that day had to offer him.

8

After that Professor Carver planned a special two-year agricultural course for him.

So far young Thomas had made his own road toward opportunity, but after his graduation opportunity came walking down a ready-made road to meet him. It came in the person of Dr. Seaman A. Knapp, the third great man to enter Thomas Campbell's life. This man had worked out a plan for farm demonstration when he was the president of Iowa State College at Ames, Iowa. It had proved to be so practical that the federal government had called him down to Washington to organize a nation-wide work under the Department of Agriculture. Up until this time he had been looking for white demonstration agents, but now he was ready to seek out colored leaders. So he had come to Tuskegee, for well he knew that no white man could "talk the lingo and get the smell of the soil" with an Alabama Negro farmer. In 1906, then, Dr. Knapp called his first Negro agent from following a two-horse plow in a Tuskegee field. The plow and the horses were probably veterans, and Booker T. Washington had purposely chosen poor soil in order to show what could be made of it. It was the man behind the plow in this case who was uncommon.

9

"Young man," said Dr. Knapp, "I want you to travel over a given territory and show the Negroes how to prepare land just as you are doing now."

And this was Thomas Campbell's first job. He was to travel about, giving other rural families a better chance than he had had when he was a boy. It was the beginning of the Negro's share in the agricultural extension service which was made national less than ten years later by the Smith-Lever Act.

But how should he travel? Booker T. Washington and Professor George Carver together worked out the answer in the Jesup Agricultural Wagon. In those days this was really a wagon, and it was designed to carry around the county a continuous exhibit of the simple things that help to improve farm life. Thomas Campbell had no assistants until he trained them, no friends until he made them; but both processes were easy for him, as they still are. Presently Mr. Campbell worked himself out of the demonstration job in the county into district and then state work, leaving a group of trained men on the road behind him. Then he worked himself out of that state and into the next, eastward to his own state of Georgia and westward to Texas. Later he was appointed an agricultural collaborator for the

United States Department of Agriculture, with two hundred and thirty agents under him.

"I confess," says Mr. Campbell, "that at the time I was puzzled as to the actual meaning of the title of agricultural collaborator." Whatever it means, his civil service rating on the job is now 94.4.

Before Mr. Campbell's work began to take him on two-thousand-mile trips from his headquarters at Tuskegee Institute, he married a classmate, Annie M. Ayers, of Virginia. Miss Ayers had been a farm girl who used to cry when her mother kept her out of school on wash day. She had worked her way through Tuskegee Institute, been trained as a nurse in Chicago, and had returned to the campus as assistant to the head nurse in the John T. Andrew Memorial Hospital. Now Mr. and Mrs. Campbell have six children, two of whom are already graduates of Tuskegee with the B.S. degree. The second son is named George Carver Campbell.

Thomas Campbell gradually made his own job into something bigger and bigger. His full official title is now "Field Agent of the Cooperative Extension Service of the United States Department of Agriculture, at work in the Gulf states for Negro farmers." Years ago the Jesup Agricultural Wagon was replaced by a truck called the Booker T. Washington Agricultural School on Wheels, the gift of thirty thousand Negro farmers of Alabama. This School on Wheels belongs to the Alabama Extension Service and represents only a fraction of the work which Mr. Campbell supervises. Yet it provides a sort of miniature picture of the kind of work that those two hundred and thirty extension agents are doing in the seven Gulf states and is therefore worth a special description.

For every trip this School on Wheels loads up with a stock of home conveniences and farm tools such as the average farmer could purchase and operate, provided he saw the point of having them. There is a set of carpenter's tools, a milk tester, spraying outfits, a Delco lighting plant, a baby's bathtub and a set of baby clothes, a sewing machine, and a full set of kitchen utensils. In addition there is a motion picture projector, a kodak, and simple playground apparatus for community games. More important, however, are the trained men and women who know what to do with all this equipment and how to show it in action.

It is a great day for any colored community when this movable school comes to town. The idea is to select some colored farmer, well liked by his neighbors, who has had a run of hard luck so that his farm is below par. The School on Wheels moves in, and the whole neighborhood becomes the class. What the neighbors do for their friend under expert supervision, they learn how to do for themselves. And what they are doing all day long in a dozen or so groups includes such jobs as whitewashing a house for a dollar and a half instead of painting it at the impossible cost of twenty-five dollars; spraying trees; building a model chicken house; canning and preserving. As Mr. Campbell reports, "Wherever it visits, the movable school seeks to leave the house and premises whitewashed; build a new poultry house or repair an old one; leave hot beds and cold frames in the garden; leave the orchard pruned, wormed and sprayed; leave shuck mats and rag mats on the floor; and, more than all, it endeavors to leave the family thrilled with the beauty and attractiveness of an old home made new, and ready to carry out any program that may provide for further transformation. In addition to these examples may be found a sanitary toilet, steps repaired, and many other improvements from which even the casual passer-by may get a lesson. This 'extensionized' home represents a 'first aid' in practical rural education, and stands as an object lesson. Frequently those who have seen the work done go back home and improve their own premises. . . . After several visits of the School on Wheels," he adds, "shacks, filth and shiftlessness gradually disappear." [1]

It would take more than the mere presence of a truck filled with modern equipment to produce a result like that among discouraged and hopeless farmers. The trained men and women who set the equipment going and make farmers believe that any of them can use it are the real cause of the transformation in many a home. No wonder Mr. Campbell says of them: "The Negro extension agents are not simply teachers in agriculture and home economics. They are that and more. They are missionaries and ambassadors of good will, engaged in a diplomatic service."

Many white people join in the work of this program, and a white judge or a school superintendent or a doctor is likely to reenforce any of the trips nowadays. It has long since been realized that there is no such thing as "white health" or "black health"; no "white economics" or "black economics." The

[1] From "Narrative Summary of Negro Extension Work, 1934," mimeographed report by Thomas M. Campbell. By permission.

problems form one great common problem, which in this case is the problem of making a better life possible in rural areas. Health, for example, is a problem common to all rural neighborhoods where unscreened houses, shallow wells and surface toilets are found together, along with monotonous food and not enough of that because of low income. As Mr. Campbell says, "The Negro agents cannot remain in this work long without viewing the problems of country life as 'one broad plain and one boundless reach of sky.'"

Thomas Campbell has his own way of introducing this matter of health to the rural people among whom he travels. He might say something like this in a country church: "There are six thousand white folks in this county and twenty-two thousand Negroes, but I'll bet that over half of those twenty-two thousand Negroes got up this morning feeling 'just tollable.' I'll bet everyone of you right here got up feeling 'just tollable.' These friends have come here today to tell you how to feel more than 'just tollable,' how to feel well, one hundred per cent well." [1] Then the doctor, white or colored, will give

[1] "Exit the Root Doctor," *Tuskegee Messenger*, March, 1932. By permission.

a practical talk and the nurse will demonstrate the best things to do to get well quickly when sickness does come.

Or Mr. Campbell may begin like this: "I've often thought that if I were some big chief"—chuckles greet this remark, since Mr. Campbell is six feet three—"I'd like to make the colored people do just as I said for five years. I'd say, No more churches till we use all the time the ones we already have. Use the schoolhouses we have nine months of the year. You can't get an education by going into a school three months and walking past it for nine. And I'd make a law that every man not having a bathtub must sell his auto and buy one. The preacher'll do the baptising for you, but he hasn't got time to do the bathing for you." [1]

No wonder that Mr. Campbell's oldest son, Thomas Campbell, Jr., went on to take a medical course at Meharry Medical College in Nashville, Tennessee, and that George Carver Campbell went to Cornell University to study farm management and agricultural economics.

Health costs money. The immediate problem,

---

[1] From "A School That Travels Around," by Mary Jenness, in the *Adult Bible Class Monthly* for April, 1929.

then, is to raise the Negro farmer's earning power to the point where he can pay off the mortgage, repair his roof, buy new farm tools, and produce food enough for his family. How is Mr. Campbell planning to do all this? In the last few years the problem of relief has complicated the situation, and yet the general outline remains the same. The general method is to continue what Booker T. Washington began and make it possible for a farmer to get the most out of the land which he works. A farmer who with trained help can raise two hundred and sixty-six bushels of sweet potatoes on soil where only forty-nine bushels have been grown before becomes a demonstration center all by himself.

From that point on, Thomas Campbell joins hands with all the agencies, colored and white, that are working to make a better home life possible in the Gulf states. It is an impressive list of state and government agents, presidents of land-grant colleges, farm organizations and civic bodies. Of course the rural preacher is on the list. For his special help the Board of Home Missions of the Methodist Episcopal Church has developed a series of summer institutes with courses in animal husbandry and agriculture as well as in theology. Mr. Campbell and members of

17

his staff manage to swing around to some of the lectures and classes.

About twenty years ago the Jeanes and Slater Funds began to work for rural schools, and now the Rosenwald schools have appeared, as will be told in later chapters. All these were powerful reenforcements for a rural betterment squad that was already on the march.

In 1930 Mr. Campbell received the Harmon Award for distinguished achievement among Negroes in the field of farming and rural life. The award included a gold medal and four hundred dollars in cash. This was one of a series of awards that had been planned as a five-year experiment by the Harmon Foundation in cooperation with the Department of Race Relations of the Federal Council of Churches. Earlier awards had been given to arouse interest in creative work done by Negroes in art, music, literature, industry, science, religion, and education. Mr. Campbell was now proving that creative work may be done in a farm extension job, and the committee felt that for that reason he should be given the award. On receiving it he quoted a farmer friend who often said, "I am glad you laks it, 'cause yo' know w'en a man do's all he kin, he ain't don' much."

Afterward, Mr. Campbell's youngest son held him up with a searching question: "What did you do to win this prize?" There may have been a bit of family emphasis on the word "you."

Mr. Campbell's answer came in the Booker T. Washington tradition, illuminated with the wide Campbell grin: "Work."

TWO

"FOR THE ONE-ROOM CABIN
SCHOOLS"

A LITTLE colored girl crouched by the fire in a dark
cabin room, studying her lessons by the light of burn-
ing pine-knots just as Lincoln used to do. Her grandfather had taught her to watch for wood-knots and
pick them up so that she might have light enough to
study after dark. After she was grown, Matilda
Moseley wrote her autobiography and told the
story of those pioneer days. "My parents had but
one lamp—and that seldom had a chimney—and they
blew it out at their eight o'clock bedtime right after
I had finished the chores. The light of this wood-
knot fire and the trudging away through all kinds of
weather enabled me to make a grade each year as a
fairly good scholar."

That grandfather had been a slave and had seen
how hard his former mistress had worked in order to
educate her four children. He remembered this later
and made up his mind that his only grandchild must

go to school, no matter what effort it cost. And it did take uncommon effort, for there in the low country in Halifax County, Virginia, none of the neighbors' children went to school regularly. The nearest school was four miles away, and the parents did not want to urge the children out in all kinds of weather. Besides, as in Thomas Campbell's case, there was nearly always some crop to be gathered. And even then, writes Mrs. Matilda Moseley Booker, "No matter how early they finished gathering their crops, few people made any attempt to send their children to school until after Christmas, notwithstanding the fact that our school term was only five months long."

Even at five years old, Matilda Moseley wanted to go to school, and her enthusiasm was catching. "After the holiday," she writes, "I with a path-full of boys and girls trotted merrily those four miles to the Staunton River School." At least it was a flat four miles.

After seven years of this school the teacher began urging the parents to send Matilda to a mission school in the next county where she had relatives— to Thyne Institute in Chase City, Virginia, a United Presbyterian school.

Matilda's mother bought her clothes with the

butter-and-egg money, but the family had no extra
cash to pay even the tiny mission fee of five dollars
a month for board and lodging. Matilda worked side
by side with her father on his farm that summer,
but farm prices just then were very low. Finally her
parents made an arrangement with a cousin whose
husband was the janitor for Thyne Institute. Matilda
might live with them if she would furnish and cook
her own food and help her cousin do the washing for
several families. So every morning the girls got up
at four o'clock, did the housework, and then helped
the janitor to make the fires in each classroom at the
school.

"Each summer," writes Mrs. Booker, "I went
home and worked on the farm with my father, helping in the corn and tobacco, and feeding and water-
ing the team. Along with this, I did most of the
housework." She did this every summer for four
years. Thereupon she taught for two years on a
temporary third-grade certificate at fifteen dollars a
month, always hoping to get back to school.

Finally, an uncle, a minister in New Brunswick,
New Jersey, came to take her back North with him
where she could earn more money. She got a job
"cooking in a boarding house with forty people and

doing all the ironing for three or four dollars a
week." In five months she had earned eighty dollars
and had saved all but nineteen cents of it. "Ten cents
I gave to the church, five cents for my first ride on a
street car, and four cents for four balls of sewing
thread to take with me to school." Her plan by this
time was to enter the Virginia Normal and Industrial Institute at Petersburg, now Virginia State College for Negroes.

Here, in 1917, Matilda Moseley entered as a work
student. She also worked through the summer vacations at the usual rate of fifteen dollars a month. She
did this for three years and also managed "to find
enough time to keep up with my class and to take
active part in all of the literary programs, the Y.W.
C.A. and everything else of note around the campus."
Even an appendicitis operation failed to prevent her
graduation, and the doctor was so impressed by her
persistence and good faith in paying him her first
earnings that he returned the money as a graduation
present.

While Matilda Moseley had been a student in
Virginia in the normal institute, something had hap-
pened which was the beginning of a new day for
Negro teachers in the rural areas of the South. In

23

1907 Anna T. Jeanes, a Philadelphia Quaker, had established the Negro Rural School Fund, Inc., a trust fund expressly for the Negro cabin schools, forgotten in out-of-the-way places. The trustees, after studying the situation, had decided to work through the rural county units and were certain that what the colored schools most needed was a trained supervisor. A beginning was made in Henrico County, Virginia, for several reasons. First, it is a small county, only thirty miles long and twelve miles broad. There were less than twenty colored schools, and there was a kindly white superintendent who went out of his way to help them as much as he could.

In the city of Richmond at that time a colored teacher lived who was doing a new kind of work entirely on her own in the Old Mountain School; it was what would now be called industrial arts teaching. Her name was Virginia E. Randolph. In 1908 Miss Randolph was called to become the pioneer Jeanes teacher; that is, the industrial arts supervisor for Henrico County. Within one month Miss Randolph had organized a Patrons' Improvement League and begun industrial arts teaching in every school she had visited.

Such was the beginning of the small, devoted army

24

of Jeanes teachers who are now at work in three hundred and thirty-nine rural counties in fifteen states of the South. Pride has been aroused to such an extent that now local funds are forthcoming at the rate of two to one to match the gifts from the trust fund. That pioneer supervisor, Virginia Randolph, is still at work in Henrico County, where in 1926 she received the Harmon Award in education.

So Matilda Moseley found herself in line for good training when she went to Henrico County as the principal of a two-teacher school. In 1911 the Little Bethel School was one of those cabin schools which Miss Randolph had not yet had time to improve. It had been an ordinary cabin about eighteen by twenty-four feet, with the door on the gabled end, two windows on each side and one in the rear. Later a shed room was added. The cabin had never been painted inside or out, and had grown black with the years. Fortunately such a state of affairs was nothing new to Miss Moseley, and she went at her job of improvement in the true missionary spirit. The white superintendent of the county schools was sympathetic and anxious to help, but he had no extra money for colored schools.

"So," writes Miss Moseley, "we gave programs

and parties and raised money enough to paint our school on the inside and whitewash it on the outside. We planted such shrubbery as we could find in the woods, and bought washbasins, a first-aid kit, a mirror, pictures for the walls, etc., which made our school look very homelike. We gave our whole life and time to the service of our people. They soon found out that four o'clock and pay-day were not our only objectives, and we found out that where there was a will there was a way. We were with the children at school five days, at the homes of our patrons in the late afternoons and on Saturdays, and in Sunday school and church services every Sunday." No wonder that such a teacher was reappointed for the next year!

Miss Moseley was presently asked to become a supervisor herself for the twenty-three colored schools in Cumberland County. She hesitated, but not because she knew that it would be a twelve-month job of continuous travel with double work in school and home. She didn't mind hard work, but she knew from watching Virginia Randolph how much the job demanded. She said frankly, "I thought it more job than I was able to fill." She knew that she would be expected to raise the money needed for blackboards and chalk, fuel and textbooks, and for all repairs on old buildings. As she improved the teachers she must raise the money to increase their salaries. She must help the women of the county to can and sew and make better homes. And she must do anything else whatever to promote the welfare of the Negroes in that county. All of this Matilda Moseley had seen Miss Randolph do, never advising anything that she could not do herself, and displaying, as a white friend writes, "a genius for doing the simple little things that make up the larger things in education and character." This particular graduate had a pioneer childhood behind her, and saw nothing to fear in a pioneer job. Miss Randolph encouraged her, and Miss Moseley agreed to try.

When Miss Moseley went to her new job in April of 1913 she found the schools already closed—a proof that the short term of from two to five months for Negro children was accepted in Cumberland County. She began her job by praying about it. Then she started on foot around the county, trudging from one community to the next, until the colored people came to value her enough to send her along "on whatever they had to ride on." She sought out the people through the Sunday school and churches and then went into their homes. The first thing she did was to teach the women and girls how to can food. "They spent very little time," she writes, "in canning anything except apples and berries and peaches. My first job then was to convince my people that vegetables, chickens, and meat as well as fruit could be canned—everything from hog chittlings to turnip greens."

By September Miss Moseley had found out that twenty-one of the twenty-three school buildings were in very bad repair, and that the length of the school term, as well as its time of starting, varied according to the local crops. In September she learned that only a few of her teachers had certificates and that many of them had finished only the fifth grade. She went after all these problems at once. Before she left the county after a seven years' stay, she had aroused the people to build eight new Rosenwald schools and to remodel thirteen old buildings. She stirred the pride of the colored parents for the first time, and the school term became seven months for Negro children—actually the same as for white children. She woke up her teachers and sent them to summer school until all but three held at least an elementary certificate. Betters teachers meant better salaries; so she

28

doubled the former salary range of ten to twenty-seven dollars a month. Then she had to raise the extra money in the colored communities, for the county school budget could not be stretched. From her summer work in the homes had come garden and canning exhibits which were a welcome feature of the fall meeting of the new County Teachers' Association. Like every Jeanes teacher, Miss Moseley had gladly invested a large part of her tiny salary in getting all these movements started.

After three years of this work Miss Moseley was married to Mr. Samuel G. Booker, but she continued with her county job. Their Christian home has become a living demonstration of what is possible for colored citizens. This is her account of it: "We had been reared on the farm and taught to save, so we bought a little home of about fourteen acres and cultivated these in our spare time. We were soon able to buy a horse and jumper"—the local term for a sulky, a coveted social distinction—"which enabled me to do my work with more ease. We took into our home orphan children to help, which made us patrons of the school." Her husband developed a general store with a filling station, which made their home the center of a progressive neighborhood.

One of the first things the Bookers did was to strengthen the local church. Miss Moseley had found it hidden away on a very bad road. She influenced the members to move it on to a good road and helped them to raise the necessary money. She adds, "Every school I have been able to remodel or build had its beginning in some church or Sunday school where I have taken pride to work irrespective of denomination." She herself is a Baptist.

After seven years in Cumberland County Mrs. Booker was called to a more responsible position as supervisor of the colored schools in Mecklenburg County, where Thyne Institute is located.

Once more Mrs. Booker found a cordial white superintendent, Mr. C. B. Green. "He never seemed to tire of the many vexing problems I brought him, and he was never too busy to spare a few minutes for me and my troubles." And that is a tribute, for the white superintendent usually has his hands full with the white schools and is only too glad to leave the colored group entirely to the Jeanes teacher. This one, however, manages to call at least once each term in every colored classroom and to meet the colored teachers in several of their teachers' meetings. Mrs. Booker, of course, would be expected to raise her own funds for such extras as a school nurse and school buses, but this county's budget did take care of repairs.

Here were new problems to be solved by prayer and persistence. First, in this large county there were forty-nine colored schools at such distances that Mrs. Booker could not inspect them all that summer, as she had to walk from one community to another. In the second place, the teaching staff was of lower grade than she had ever found. Of the seventy-nine teachers, only five held even elementary certificates, and fifty-one had nothing but local permits. "I pled with my teachers to go to summer school," she writes. "I arranged extension courses for them, and thereby managed to get most of the old stand-bys in the ark before the flood came." Now, fifteen years later, that county has fifty-six colored schools with one hundred and nineteen teachers. Fewer than a third have only an elementary certificate, more than half have two years of training beyond high school, and eighteen have a college degree. The principal of the new county training school holds a Master's degree.

The most exciting part of this story, however, is the story of the new Rosenwald schools. Of the original forty-nine buildings, fifteen were in fair condition, but there was not one Rosenwald school in the six hundred square miles of the county. People hadn't even heard of the Rosenwald Fund. Mrs. Booker promptly told them how Julius Rosenwald of Chicago, a distinguished Jew, had celebrated his fiftieth birthday in 1912 by establishing a fund to improve rural education for Negroes. This fund would match whatever the local people, colored and white, could raise, and would also plan the school building. Once they grasped the idea, the Negroes set to work to raise money, and at the end of four terms they had actually won five new Rosenwald schools.

"By this time the people all over the county had the building fever," writes Mrs. Booker, "and I was wanted in every community to help make suggestions for raising the money. I asked the county school board for another supervisor to help me put this building program over while the fever was on the people. The board asked if I could do the work if my salary was raised enough for me to pay someone to take me around rather than walking and waiting for trains. I at once told them that a gallon bucket was considered full when it held all it could hold, that more salary wouldn't make two persons out of me, and that two were needed for this large county. They finally decided to put on another worker, and asked me to recommend the person." The colored people of the county not long afterward gave Mrs. Booker a car for her faithful service.

Now Mecklenburg County boasts of better school equipment for Negroes than any other county in Virginia. More than half of the fifty-six school buildings are almost brand new, and sixteen of these are Rosenwald schools. Five new buildings are needed, and five more need repair, but that record sets a new low for rural colored schools. What is more, the county superintendent feels that what Mrs. Booker and her friend have done has raised the whole educational standard and outlook of the colored people. This is what he writes: "Our colored patrons contribute generously of their limited funds for their schools. They raised something like five or six thousand dollars during depression years. They are operating four or five school buses for high school students; they have just made a contribution of five hundred dollars for a dental clinic for each colored school; and they have improved sanitary conditions and ways of living in their homes. In fact, *they are becoming a new race*. Taken as a whole, we have a splendid colored citizenship in this county. On the

33

colored children we are spending out of the levies five times as much as the colored taxes amount to in this county."

And here is what this modest product of a mission school says about herself: "I owe my success as a worker to my heavenly Father for his strength, protection and divine guidance day by day; to the strong support of my teachers, patrons and friends, and the fine spirit of cooperation and earnest support given me by my most honored superintendents and school board members. Without this help I would not have had the courage to attempt many of my tasks."

THREE

A CITY PASTOR

THERE WERE a hundred boys and girls of five races
in the vested choir that came marching in processional
down the aisle of a great city church. The oldest of
them was not over eighteen years old. They were in
groups, each wearing the choir robes of its own
church. One group was wearing all black, and another wore white surplices. Then came a group wearing dark blue with light blue, another in white wool
with short fitted capes, and finally a group in dark
red with white. These Japanese, Italian, Czecho-
slovakian, Negro, and other American children came
marching and singing together, "Joyful, Joyful, We
Adore Thee." Eight city churches were uniting in the
annual observance of Race Relations Sunday in the
Madison Avenue Church in New York City. The
Negro group was one of the six children's choirs of
St. James Presbyterian Church.

A reporter who was interested enough to make a
trip to St. James Church that week had to wait for

nearly two hours before he could catch the busy minister and get some information about those famous choirs. He was never bored for a moment while he waited in the church office, for he soon realized that the life of a church of a thousand members was flowing through it.

This eight-by-ten room with stained glass windows and paneled door is crowded with two office desks, a filing cabinet and an overflowing table. The telephone rings constantly. If it is an inquiry about a job, the secretary has the name and address of many employment offices on a bulletin board beside her, and she knows that the pastor stands ready to act as sponsor and reference. She gets the date for her endless letter-writing from a calendar given by the American League against War and Fascism or from one given by the Dunbar National Bank, named after Paul Laurence Dunbar and the only bank in New York City in which Negroes are employed as clerks, tellers and officers. Above one desk hangs the Award for Distinguished Service in Race Relations, given to St. James Church by the New York Presbytery in 1933. On the side table are piles of folders and leaflets. Many of these are such as come to all live city churches: material from city, state and national federations of churches; mission study folders from the national church headquarters; announcements about the Emergency Peace Campaign and the American Youth Act. Other papers reflect the special interests of this church; there are publications of the United Aid for Ethiopia and the National Negro Congress; there is the bulletin of National Negro Week and a pamphlet entitled "Young Black America Looks at Fascism." A trustees' report shows a budget balanced by a hair. The money was raised largely by the every-member-canvass, but a poster of the "Win One" Bible class shows how part of the money was raised in another way. That class put on an entertainment that was good enough by professional standards to warrant being given in a public auditorium.

All this time the minister has been seeing one person after another in his study or in any unoccupied spot that he can find. More people form a waiting-line in the church pews. Half of them have come about getting jobs. Several are young people in trouble of some sort. One distinguished looking man is a visiting minister. One has come to collect a bill. Another is a salesman; and yet another brings a report of the milk cooperative in the Dunbar Apartments, of which we shall hear more later. No one could watch this procession of persons without wanting to know more about the minister, the engineer who keeps all these currents of power in action. His name is William Lloyd Imes. This name is in *Who's Who in America* for 1936; it has been in *Who's Who in Colored America* for some years.

Dr. Imes's father and grandfather were farmers in Pennsylvania, born free, though in the time of slavery. The father worked his way westward to Oberlin College in the seventies, and there in nine years he worked his way through college and seminary. There, too, he met his wife, who had been a slave in West Virginia, "sold South" but brought back North by Union soldiers as contraband of war. In Oberlin she secured the equivalent of a high school education. Presently this couple were sent down to Memphis, Tennessee, as home missionaries under the American Missionary Association. Here William Lloyd Imes was born. The father was put in charge of a tiny mission chapel for Negroes, and in twelve years made it a self-supporting church. "He didn't believe in permanent missions," says his son; "—the kind that keep a church dependent on someone higher up."

After this experience came a succession of pastorates through the South, all poorly paid, and all cruelly difficult under post-war conditions. "But I am glad I had a home missionary bringing-up," says Dr. Imes. "There were always books, you see, and a high standard of life, and trained parents. My father coached me in preparation for college."

The father died when the son was half through Knoxville College, a United Presbyterian missionary institution in eastern Tennessee. From this time on, the boy earned his own way completely. He transferred to Fisk University in Nashville, Tennessee, from which he was graduated in 1910. He stayed on to get a Master's degree in sociology before going North to Union Theological Seminary in New York City. Here he worked his way by singing in the choir, playing the organ at Labor Temple, leading boys' clubs, and acting as student minister in various pulpits. In spite of all his extra work he won merit scholarships, standing usually in the second honor group. Many of the graduates of those years live now in or near New York City, and in 1934 Dr. Imes was elected president of their alumni association.

During his senior year in the seminary, William Lloyd Imes won a second Master's degree; this one was from Columbia University and was likewise in the field of sociology, for he realized that a trained pastor needs to know all he can about the ways in which people live and get along together.

Then the seminary graduate went out to a mission chapel in Plainfield, New Jersey, where, he says, he learned enough to make up for the lack of an adequate salary. He was the pastor of one of three mission chapels supported by a white Presbyterian church. Members of his congregation were mostly servants and unfortunately had a "slave attitude" that made them yield to white people even when the whole right and law was on their side. For instance, their chapel had been built near the white section of the town and far away from the section where the Negroes lived. As a result the minister had to go back and forth on a bicycle. Finally the supporting church bought the house next door to the chapel for a parsonage, but when several white families objected, the church yielded to the prejudice and agreed to sell it again. That happened in war time when the pastor was on leave of absence for Y.M. C.A. work at Camp Merritt. "My home was sold from under me while I was away helping to make the world safe for democracy," says Dr. Imes with a smile. "Knowing what I do now, I would have fought such a thing," he adds; "but then I was young and green." During this pastorate he had married a young Northern woman whose family had been free for two generations on the mother's side and seven generations on the father's side. Her mother's father ran away from his master as a boy of fifteen, ragged and penniless, and made his way North to freedom. The Imes children are as proud of him as of another ancestor who was an Indian chief, for, as Mrs. Imes asks them, "What children of any race in America today would have the spunk to do such a thing?"

In his next pastorate in the Lombard Central Church in Philadelphia, the minister found a more self-respecting congregation living on a better economic level, with an independent life of their own. During his six-year pastorate they purchased a four-thousand-dollar parsonage, paid all their debts, and still had a building fund of several thousand dollars in the bank. Their minister was presently asked to serve on the interracial commission organized by the Society of Friends. At that time the committee was agitated by a move toward segregating Negro education by the establishment of a separate state normal school for Negroes. They lost, and segregation won.

But, as Dr. Imes says, "I'd rather lose a fight like that than never make it." Today some of the public schools of Philadelphia are for Negroes only, and some are mixed, but the Negro girl can teach only in a Negro school. "The white girl at graduation," says Dr. Imes, "knows that she is considered prepared to teach, but the Negro girl knows that she is considered prepared to teach only Negroes! The situation is not fair to either one. The white girl has no interracial competition for her job in the mixed schools, and the Negro girl has no interracial competition for her job in the Negro schools. Therefore, neither of the girls is held up to her best. In view of the new Pennsylvania Civil Rights law, if I lived there now I'd take my taxpayer's receipts and bring suit in the civil court. Somebody will do that sometime, for it's the right thing to do under the state law. What would you do if you were a Negro in such circumstances?" In all his activities of this sort the congregation supported their minister.

St. James Presbyterian Church in New York City called Dr. Imes in 1925. This New York church had grown out of a small group that began meeting in a downtown home. That was in 1895, under the Rev. Pierce B. Thompkins. In the spring of 1936 St.

James Church celebrated the forty-first anniversary
of that beginning. The congregation had made suc-
cessive moves uptown until they reached the southern
edge of Harlem. Under Dr. Imes's leadership the
church was soon filled to the bursting point, and arrangements were made to take over its present building, then just being vacated by a white congregation.
The square brick tower of St. James Church rises on
the northwest corner of West 141st Street and St.
Nicholas Avenue. This avenue forms a main highway
north and south, separating the neighborhood of City
College on the west from the most crowded quarter
of Harlem on the east. New apartment houses rise
on the hill to the west of the church, and old-law
tenements may be seen within a block in the opposite
direction. Families from both areas will be found in
the Sunday morning congregation; the washerwoman
and the well dressed doctor's or lawyer's wife sit side
by side.

Though the church auditorium with its three bal-
conies and East Parlor seats a thousand people, the
late-comer may have to sit in a chair in the aisle.
Even there he can join in a dignified worship be-
neath stained glass windows with a setting and a
service that will compare favorably with the best

43

churches in the city. The organist, wearing a pink-bordered hood which signifies his degree of Doctor of Music, is Dr. Melville Charlton, for many years the organist at the Sunday morning service at Union Theological Seminary. The vested choir probably practised till midnight last Friday, and they may have put five months of work on the anthem before their director was satisfied. "They must sing the best music accurately and intelligently." That is his standard. So the congregation is trained to appreciate the great church music, including works of the Negro composers Samuel Coleridge-Taylor and Harry T. Burleigh and others. In the congregation even the humblest worshiper can enjoy the perfect tone and rhythm, and on the platform the minister, himself an organist trained at Fisk University, follows every measure. On special occasions he wears the gown and scarlet hood of his Doctor of Divinity degree from Lincoln University. His sermon is certain to be simple enough for the most unskilled laborer and challenging enough for the college student, and it is always delivered with a passion and power that sets them both tingling.

Anyone who goes walking through this church toward the end of the Sunday school hour hears snatches of well sung chants and hymns floating all about, for every department in the Sunday school has its own vested choir, with week-day practice. The Bluebirds Choir is composed of the smallest children. The primary children's choir is called the Canaries, and four older choirs are named for Roland Hayes, Nathaniel L. Dett, Harry T. Burleigh, and Samuel Coleridge-Taylor. There is a boys' glee club besides. Every second Sunday of the month from December to June these choirs join in an afternoon church service. Every now and then guest choirs join them from other churches, sometimes white and sometimes colored. These choirs from St. James Church are well known in New York City, where they take part in an annual junior choir festival held in Riverside Church, of which Dr. Harry Emerson Fosdick is pastor. On Race Relations Sunday, they have for several years marched in processional with the vested choirs of six races at the Madison Avenue Presbyterian Church. One who listened to the Harry T. Burleigh choir practice before Easter will never forget how the director of church school music lifted a group of intermediate boys and girls right out of themselves, tired and restless though many of them were. At the piano, without need of words, she let

45

the accompaniment to a great Negro spiritual sing its way over and over again deep down into their minds:

"He arose, He arose, He arose from the dead!
And the Lord shall bear my spirit home."

No wonder that choir members are given a church credit for work equal to the week-day classes of the church school! As the pastor says to parents, "Church music is an essential part of a child's religious education."

The regular week-day school has a varied program emphasizing the Bible and missions. The departments alternate between these subjects, so that both Bible and missionary materials are studied each year.

An example of the practical nature of the missionary teaching in this church can be seen in what happened in an intermediate class studying Latin America. The class had just been told the ancient Mexican legend of the Fair God, that fair-skinned patron who taught his brown people useful arts of living and left them with the promise that he would come again. Centuries later came the Spanish invaders, who were met with a warm welcome because their skin was fair. The welcome was undeserved, for the foreign soldiers turned out to be ruthless conquerors, as unlike

46

the Fair God as possible. After telling the story, the teacher proceeded to use it as the basis for bringing out the fact that people should be judged by what they do, and not by what they happen to look like.

"If you stop to think," said the teacher, "you can see that those Indians didn't think their leader was divine just because his skin happened to be light. They thought so because he was good and taught them good ways of living. The conquerors had light complexions, too, but they turned out to be anything but good. So the Indians learned that color of skin hasn't a thing to do with what you really are. Some fair people are good, and some are bad; and the same holds true of the brown races."

This week-day department earned thirty dollars for the church budget in 1936 by the home-talent circus it gives each year. Indeed, in the past few years, every organization in that church has done all it could, and then more, to meet the heavy bills for insurance and mortgage payments, for coal in a church that is used every day of the week, and for similar necessities. When the church calendar carries an appeal to every auxiliary to "sacrifice five dollars more this month for the kitchen equipment," the word "more" tells only half the story. It is manpower and woman-power that has kept that church driving ahead, with uncounted hours of volunteer work, hard and heavy, on all sorts of tasks. In eight years the congregation has raised $33,000 toward its building fund in addition to its yearly budget of $15,000, as St. James is a self-supporting congregation. Every one of the fifteen organizations among the adults in St. James Church—including missionary, musical, and literary societies, as well as organizations for mutual aid and for medical aid—is a hard-working church auxiliary. And what is true of most Negro rural churches is true here: the whole social life of most of the members flows through their church. The rural church can never depend on the white community for social services, and this city church is as independent as it can be in a time of depression. "Mutual aid, that's what a church is for," says the pastor. His congregation know that too, for though possibly a third of them have had to go on relief, it is their church which cares for them as individuals, by guidance, advice, and practical assistance with funds as far as possible, through the board of deacons.

Not that St. James Church draws back from its community! You might attend a prayer meeting in

48

the spring, after the annual school of missions is over, and find yourself signing a petition against militarism in the public schools, or one for better housing in Harlem. This congregation took seriously a recent sermon in which Dr. Imes asked: "Are there no children in your neighborhood who have no place for wholesome play, for safety from physical and moral dangers and from indecent and dangerous housing? And would you dare not to do the least thing about it? If you have the mind of Christ, my friend, you will try!"

The young people study their community as well. The members of the Six o'Clock Circle, which meets on Sunday evenings, have been making a survey of the liquor shops in that area and have found that the number is far in excess of the law. They have been learning how to work for their legal rights in this matter. Also such questions as these have occupied them: "Why get an education when we find no chance to use it? What type of job should we train for? Why go out of our way to train for what we may never be able to get? Why not go into a racket? Where shall we live when no decent quarters are open at a price we can pay?"

A hopeful note entered the discussions when a girl

who lives in the Paul Laurence Dunbar apartments told the group about the success of the new milk cooperative of which Dr. Imes is the first president. She gleefully quoted the slogan coined in 1936: "One year old—and it walks!" Within a year Harlem's Own Cooperative, Inc., paid all expenses, engaged a full-time worker, paid four per cent on its capital, and saved $125, which was rebated to the twenty members—all out of a turnover of fewer than a thousand quarts a week. The leading New York milk companies did not surrender the tiny market gracefully, and the manager is convinced that the venture could never have won out without Dr. Imes's strong leadership. His young people are proud of the fact that he is an effective leader in such situations, because he commands an audience of thousands of people, white and colored.

Some of the young people's discussions have been helped forward by a Fellowship Student from Union Theological Seminary, assigned to his own church for boys' work as a part of his training for the Christian ministry. He was born in this city and brought up in St. James Sunday school. His mother is secretary of the board of deacons. The pastor has taken the greatest delight in encouraging his training, and the church furnishes a modest fellowship stipend.

One more story suggested in a glance around the church office deserves a paragraph. Why did St. James Presbyterian Church receive that award for distinguished service in race relations? Because two or three ministers in the New York Presbytery got together and determined to lead their parishes in the direction of better race relations. "The award should be divided with the Madison Avenue Presbyterian Church of which Dr. George Buttrick is pastor," says Dr. Imes. "Not only have our children and young people held friendly and neighborly services together, but we have also exchanged pulpits at a Sunday service, each taking our choir and organist along." A similar exchange has been made with Dr. Allan Chalmers at Broadway Tabernacle Church. These ministers joined with a few others in the city ministers' conference to stand together for better conditions after the terrible Harlem riots of 1935.

"We are not battling with the facts just for our church community," Dr. Imes said on one occasion; "we are battling for the Christian ideal of life." With this purpose he serves on the board of such organizations as the National Association for the Advancement of Colored People, the New York

Urban League, and the Race Relations Department of the Federal Council of Churches of Christ in America. He has reached the general public as a co-author of several books, among which are *What I Believe*, which includes statements by Harry Emerson Fosdick, Henry Sloane Coffin, and other nationally known church leaders, and the volume, *Best Sermons, Book Four*, edited by Joseph Fort Newton.

The Christian ideal of life as he sees it includes the ideal of peace. When Italy began the invasion of Ethiopia he led a parade of 20,000 people for the American League against War and Fascism. His radio address for the peace action committee of the New York Federation of Churches was a strong plea for "putting away from our schools, churches, business houses, factories, labor unions, newspapers, and radios . . . all those things that hurt and offend our fellow-men—not simply one class or one race of men, but all classes and all races. It is much more to the point that white men and black men should together fight against poverty, crime, disease and ignorance than that they should fight each other."

FOUR

A SOCIAL WORKER FOR BLIND AMERICANS

LILLIAN PROCTOR's story begins in Atlanta early in this century when a young Congregational minister was striking out on a new path among Negroes. The Reverend Henry H. Proctor was the first colored pastor of the First Congregational Church, following two white preachers. He and his wife, both graduates of Fisk University, had gone to Atlanta to make this home mission church self-supporting, but he was soon doing much more than that. He was making the little struggling church a center for social service, which no American city provided in those days for its Negro community. He became a towering figure in the city, well known among both races and liked and trusted outside of colored circles. Suddenly the Atlanta riots of 1906 broke out. The depression of that year had caused racial feeling to run high, and some of the Atlanta newspapers had deliberately kept it high. After two days of terror and havoc, Dr. Proctor went with a Negro and a white friend of influence to certain editors and convinced them that the welfare of the whole city, not only of the fifty thousand Negroes but of the hundred thousand whites, was in their hands. They could fan the flames as they were doing till nobody would feel safe, or they could report that the best Negroes cared as much for the reputation of the city as the best whites. The editors agreed to change their policy. Next Dr. Proctor brought together some of the best white and colored citizens to plan for the security of the whole city. The result was a tide of good will toward the colored group, during which the present building of the First Congregational Church was erected, including rooms for a gymnasium, the first library for Negroes in Atlanta, several clubs, and a business school. Out of that church presently grew the first bank for Negroes and the first Negro insurance organization, and presently a modern office building owned and used by Negro business and professional men.

Meanwhile Mrs. Proctor, though "majoring on the job at home," as she says, had started a tiny mission which grew into the first public kindergarten in Atlanta. "With five children," she says, "I was not responsible for the needs of the colored community, but I was responsive to them." During this time the father was traveling throughout the country, meeting outstanding people who came to visit his home later on. As a result, writes his daughter Lillian, "the children in our family became accustomed very early to meeting white and colored persons of culture, education and wide interests."

An exceptional colored home like this might enjoy such contacts, but at the same time it was surrounded by an entirely different social custom. Dr. Proctor was by this time known and loved all over the city, but that did not change the fact that there was no public high school for colored children. He had to pay tuition for his two sons and three daughters in the high school maintained by Atlanta University. The children had to take long daily rides on a trolley, where they were permitted to sit only on the rear seats. Lillian fiercely resented these and other social restrictions. She resolved to study very hard and see if she could work her way through and out of such limitations. Her father made a wider life possible for his children by giving all five of them college and professional training. "I can't leave them any money," he used to say, "but I can give them as much education as they can take. If I left them money, they wouldn't know how to use it well without trained minds. I want to give them what they will need for life." Two of his daughters are now teachers and one is a social worker; one son is a dentist and the other a lawyer. All five have been successful in their professional work.

The family moved from Atlanta to Brooklyn, New York, in 1920, when Lillian Proctor was a senior at Fisk University. There she had worked intensely hard and was to graduate with the highest honors, but she had not been entirely happy. Fisk University, to be sure, is like an island of security, a self-contained campus within a Southern city, where Negro students may live a life all their own. However, many of the students resent the fact that as soon as they graduate and go forth into business or industry, they will meet discrimination at many points. They are asking bitter questions. Lillian Proctor was not an exception. In fact, as the daughter of superior parents, she was especially sensitive to that kind of discrimination that takes no account of culture and personal status but centers on color alone. Fortunately, one colored professor whom she especially respected because he knew his subject, was the very one who was most noted for working easily with white professors on the staff. He stuck to the attitude, in spite of criticism from both races, that people are people, colored or white; some of both kinds are better than others, and each person has to be judged for himself. *"Some white people are fine,"* he insisted, knowing how difficult it may be for a sensitive Negro girl to admit the point. He said to Miss Proctor again and again: "If you permit these things —every snub, every symptom of racial arrogance— to hurt you, you will lead a very miserable life."

A year or so before Lillian Proctor's graduation something started in Atlanta which began to cut under the root of racial difficulties. In 1918, shortly after the Armistice, the Commission on Interracial Cooperation was founded. At that time racial hatreds were running high all over the country as the colored groups came back from the war and their first taste of a broader experience. They had enjoyed something like equal treatment in France, and now they were less patient with the same old restrictions at home. It was no accident that the first attempt at the solution appeared in Atlanta, where Dr. Henry Proctor had pointed out the way a dozen years before. If white and Negro people understood each other, he had insisted, they would not fight, and the best

57

of each group would try to do the right thing if they knew what it was. On that principle the Commission on Interracial Cooperation was founded, with head-quarters in Atlanta. Similar committees were quickly set up in several Southern states. Today there are committees of this sort in practically every state in the South, and about eight hundred local ones. "When the white minister knows the colored minister as well as the white bootlegger knows the colored bootlegger—when the best of both races know each other as well as the worst do now—then the South can work out her own problems." This statement is often made by Mr. R. B. Eleazer, the educational director of the commission. Time has proved him right.

Meanwhile, the daughter of the man whose tem-porary solution had thus been made permanent was facing the question, "After graduation, what?" Lil-lian Proctor knew only that she did not want to teach, partly because teaching was the only job usually open to a Negro girl. One other possibility offered itself. That was to take the examination given by the National Urban League, an organization which, among other things, promotes social service among Negroes. According to the notice posted in all Negro colleges, the winners would receive scholarships for training for social work. These scholarships covered tuition and also provided fifty dollars a month. Lillian Proctor was one of that year's winners. She was to go to the University of Chicago, to the Graduate School of Social Service Administration, for courses in public welfare, social investigation, and community work. Here she began to find herself. Her parents being what they were, it was not strange that she should discover ability in this line.

The National Urban League is an interracial organization with white and colored people on the executive board. They agree that poor living conditions have something to do with making poor citizens, and they try to improve Negro citizenship by working on such matters as better housing, more playgrounds, and a fair chance at employment. They also encourage colored social workers by such scholarships as the one which Miss Proctor had secured on merit. Now that she knew something about the organization, she could not help seeing that colored and white people could work together for a common cause. There were people who were actually doing it. It really was possible, then, just as her former professor at Fisk University had insisted. Dr. Henry

Proctor's daughter was actually seeing one of her father's dreams come true. So she accepted the Urban League scholarship which she had fairly earned, and went off to study social work at the University of Chicago.

There Miss Proctor proceeded to make a fine record. The dean of women says that the school is proud of the unusual record that Miss Proctor has made since then. First, she took the daring step of seeking for a job with the United Charities of Chicago, a white organization for social work. The officials hesitated, partly because she was under twenty-five, the usual minimum age, and partly because at that time there was only one colored case worker on any large welfare agency in the city. Still, Miss Proctor's school record had been so good that she was finally employed, "on probation for four months." Later on, she could afford to smile when told that "the entire social work world of Chicago had watched with bated breath" to see what would happen. To be sure, it is no easy job for any strange woman to win the confidence of a family to the point where they will let her help them through trouble. If the family is white and the worker is colored, then she will need more than average tact to get at the truth and to win the family's confidence. Fortunately for Miss Proctor, she had her father's ability to take people as people, even when they were unable to return the compliment. The result was that after the probation period, she found herself a welcome member of the staff. The girl who while she was growing up had suffered so keenly from the slights of white people was now in a position to help people of any race with her skill and training. And in Chicago she found the mixture of races to be expected in any large city. It was her job, like a nurse's, to look past the accidents of race and color straight into the needs of human beings.

For three and a half years Miss Proctor did what is called social case work; that is, she made use of every possible resource in order to help one person after another out of any kind of trouble. By and by she realized that she had gone as far as she could go without further training. It wasn't a better salary that she wanted so much as it was a chance to grow. She learned of the scholarships offered by the Commonwealth Fund and sent her application to the New York School of Social Work. By this time the United Charities in Chicago valued her enough to suggest a year's leave of absence, rather than let her resign.

However, she decided that the time had come to burn her bridges, and so she resigned.

The Commonwealth Fund was established through a private fortune to provide scholarships for training workers to help children in trouble, whether in school or at home or in the juvenile courts. These scholarships are open to college graduates who have had at least two years of experience in social work. In the New York School of Social Work no set examination faces the candidates because, as one of the staff confessed, "We couldn't figure out any kind of examination that would tell us what we wanted to know about the students." Instead, candidates are asked to describe themselves according to a certain outline. On a recent outline something like this was included: "Describe those characteristics of yours which you would expect to be of value to you in doing social work. Describe a situation which you think shows some of these characteristics in action."

No amount of skill in bluffing through examinations would get a student past anything like that. Also, the answers would have nothing more to do with the color of skin than with the color of eyes. A person would have to be chosen on merit, and on that basis Lillian Proctor won. In fact, she was one of fourteen students chosen from a hundred applicants from all over the country. She is remembered at this school as an attractive and well dressed girl, a quiet but eager student, and one likely to grow. She is also remembered because she insisted that she wanted to be able to decide whether she would do social work among Negroes or among whites. Not that she had any objection to working with a Negro agency, but she did not wish to be thus limited. One member of the school's staff pointed out that she would always find herself at a disadvantage in competing with white workers for positions. Another reminded her that the need for social work among Negroes is far greater than among whites. What a pity it would be, he pointed out, if the very few trained colored workers went into the field of lesser need! Miss Proctor still replied that she wanted to be able to choose for herself. As it turned out, she chose to accept a job in Washington, D. C., where she was to work with colored children, under the research department of the public school system.

Work with retarded colored children was just being started at the time and the plans were just being made. Miss Proctor worked out an outline of procedure which was so simple and so good that it

is still being followed. She went after the answers
to questions something like these: How far is this
child behind the normal grade for his age and why?
What has been happening in his family? How has
he been getting along in school and home up to this
time? What is his mental capacity? What can he do
now in school, considering his own ability and that
of other children of his age?

Miss Proctor's job was not only to find the answers
to some of these questions but also to make recommendations to the public school teacher and to show
her what might be done to help a retarded child.
At the same time she was working on the first study
ever made of a group of superior colored children.
What she wanted to know was this: Do superior
colored children have a better chance for normal,
happy lives than the average colored child? Through
the public school system she secured the names of
thirty children of the highest rating. All but four of
them were known to be from two to eight years ahead
of their grades in mental ability, and all but four of
them had already skipped at least one grade. She
proceeded to study their homes and their social experiences. She was forced to conclude that these children were not getting what a child needs for a nat-

ural growth in confidence. There were many school contests which they were not allowed to enter. They were welcome at entertainments and concerts if these were sponsored by colored people, but not otherwise. In the department stores they were not allowed to handle toys which they had just seen white children handling. As a result some of them were already oppressed with a sense of undeserved inferiority. The brightest of them were asking, "Why can't we do what other children do?" Their parents had no answer to make except: "You are colored." As a trained social worker, Miss Proctor felt certain that many of these children would grow up bitter and unhappy because so many normal opportunities and privileges were denied them.

All this time the United Charities in Chicago had been trying to get Miss Proctor back on their staff. They could not match the excellent Washington salary with its regular increases. However, they knew that she wanted to finish work for her Master's degree at the University of Chicago, and so they were still hoping she would come back as a worker. She did return in 1929—to marry a doctor. Later the United Charities asked her to be the acting superintendent of a certain district during the absence of its white supervisor. It was the first time that a colored woman had ever held such a position in Chicago, though by that time several colored women were acting as heads of smaller bureaus or sections of welfare work in city or county. In one sense Miss Proctor's success had had nothing to do with the other appointments, for each worker had to make good on her own merits. But it must have been easier for those who made the appointments to choose Negroes now, since the first one appointed had so well justified the faith placed in her.

In 1931, still using her maiden name for professional purposes, Lillian Proctor took a civil service examination. With a high record, she was at once appointed to the position she holds now as supervisor of the Blind Relief Service, Cook County Bureau of Public Welfare. There she found herself the head of a staff of twenty-three workers, three of whom were colored. "I can assure you she would not be there," writes a Chicago Y.M.C.A. secretary, "if she did not deserve to be, and unless she had much above the amount of ability required to serve such a bureau successfully." It proved to be a job of pioneer work in bringing up to date a bureau which had somehow been allowed to lag far behind the most modern methods in social work. In spite of opposition, many innovations were put quietly through because Miss Proctor had the training to know what should and could be done for the blind people of the county, both colored and white.

In the year of Miss Proctor's marriage her father was listed in *Who's Who in America*, an honor given to fewer than a hundred Negroes. The seed of interracial cooperation which he had planted more than twenty years ago had grown and spread to his honor.

Lillian Proctor's husband, Dr. Arthur D. Falls, is the chairman of the Chicago Interracial Commission of the Chicago Urban League, a branch of the National Urban League. This local commission has taken a positive stand for equality of opportunity for Negroes in many different situations. For instance, it has made a long and steady fight against discrimination in the public schools. It has brought the best of the two races together in church, civic, and business groups. Just now it is bringing them together through the Consumers' Cooperative Movement, having started two small study groups which it is hoped will develop into buying clubs later on. One of its activities, carried on through ten years of patient work, has borne fruit at last. That is, the public bathing beaches have been opened to all the races of the city. The decision to do this was important because it recognized the right of colored citizens who pay taxes to have privileges for their children. Now Dr. Falls may take his wife and son to enjoy a swim whenever they wish, just as white citizens do.

The most unusual thing about Lillian Proctor's life is that many forces have combined to help a competent person do a good job. It is because of her home, plus her college, plus her contact with national social organizations, that this Negro woman has made good without asking favors. She illustrates what a Negro may become when he is allowed what he really wants, according to Mrs. Mary McLeod Bethune, a widely known Negro leader in education.

Mrs. Bethune says, "The Negro asks simply for a fair chance to develop, unfold, possess, and live as other American citizens. He seeks no special consideration; only to be dealt with as a man. He does not wish to become a white man or a yellow man; he is entirely content to be himself; but he does desire the opportunity to become the best of which he is capable." Miss Proctor is one of an increasing number of well trained workers who are capable of helping white people as well as colored.

FIVE

A NEGRO COOPERATIVE MAKES GOOD

A YOUNG Negro Baptist of Philadelphia was writing
for advice to the National Negro Business Men's
League, founded by Booker T. Washington. "Seven
young men," he wrote, "have organized to promote
some sort of business enterprise. All of us are young
men earning from fifteen to twenty dollars a week.
We have organized to try to make money for each
other; we realize that we cannot get very far indi-
vidually, and so we have decided to pool our energies."

This letter was written in 1928. In 1936 when
Toyohiko Kagawa of Japan went to talk with the
ministers of Philadelphia he found that this group of
young men had ploughed straight through the depression and produced one of the four most successful Negro cooperative ventures in the United States.
The store which they had organized and were running was Exhibit A of the very thing that Kagawa
had come to this country to talk about: consumers'

cooperation. The fact was that this little group, soon after organizing, had discovered Kagawa's writings and had ever since been working to prove Kagawa's certainty that cooperation is a Christian way of doing business, and, more than that, is a Christian way of living.

The story is typical of what any group with energy and persistence can do. But if the group are colored, they must have a double share of these qualities because they would practically always have to start without capital. These seven young Negroes were originally hunting for nothing more than financial security for themselves. Later the depression came on, and before long eighty-five per cent of the Negroes of Philadelphia were unemployed and on relief. The Negro is always at the bottom of the workers' scale; he must take the poorest paid jobs and is the first to be dropped in hard times. By this time these young Baptists, with others added to their group, had discovered that consumers' cooperation is more than merely a way to save money.

Who is the Negro leader of this group who had the grit to hang on, learning as he went along? His name is Lewis E. Anthony. He was born in St. Louis. In 1922 he entered Lincoln University, Pennsylvania, the oldest college for Negroes in the country, founded by the United Presbyterians in 1854. He transferred to Temple University in Philadelphia, and graduated in 1926. He had majored in the social sciences, but like many educated Negroes could find no work in line with his training. He went from one job to another, an odd assortment which at least showed him many sides of the business world. He was a clerk in an insurance office, a factory hand, a laundry sorter, a butler in a private family, and later the manager of three apartment houses. From one point of view his most important job was in Chicago, in a coffee shop in the Loop, where the patrons were Finnish. Naturally they kept talking about the cooperative movement, but Lewis only laughed at them then. He did not yet realize that Finnish immigrants had been the pioneers of the cooperative movement in this country. But some of their words stuck in his mind. He remembered them later when he was the manager of a chain store in Philadelphia.

Suddenly the thing happened that was to make Lewis Anthony the founder and manager of a Negro cooperative store. He discovered George Schuyler's column in one of the best-known Negro newspapers, the Pittsburgh *Courier*. George Schuyler was using

71

his column in 1930 to urge young Negroes to try the cooperative movement. He outlined a nation-wide plan for organization, and he explained cooperative principles. At that time he saw little more in the movement than a means to power for an oppressed race, a financial kind of power that would compel the respect of whites. But one paragraph on his enrolment blank caught this young Christian's eye:

"I, too, want to see something done to give the younger generation hope and faith and the courage to look forward to a brighter future. I, too, want to be a pioneer, a charter member of the Young Negroes' Cooperative League."

Whereupon Lewis Anthony did as George Schuyler suggested, and called a few of his friends together for a year's study of cooperative principles. One member, a tailor, offered the back room of his shop. The room had nothing in it except a two-foot table and an old chair or two. Here a few boys and girls came once a week, and under Lewis Anthony's direction they settled down to real study of how to become cooperators. Eagerly they pored over the principles worked out by twenty-eight poor weavers of Rochdale, England, nearly one hundred years ago. They learned that every cooperative buying or selling business which has followed the principles has succeeded, and that every one which has dropped even one of them has failed. They decided that they could not afford to neglect any of the following rules:

1. One vote for each member, no matter how many shares he may buy in the business.
2. Equal membership rights for men and women.
3. Cash sales at the prevailing local prices.
4. Profits distributed to members (after meeting all expenses) in proportion to purchases.
5. Interest on capital restricted to a fixed rate, usually five per cent or less, with the first claim on profits.
6. Regular and frequent meetings to discuss business and receive suggestions for improvement.
7. Accounts properly kept and audited, and balance sheets regularly presented to members.

The idea which Americans have added to these English discoveries has been the one of setting aside a certain amount of the profits in order to educate more people in the principles of cooperation. It would be several years, however, before Mr.

Anthony's group got so far as having any profits at all. In the meantime they could see how the fairness of these principles to all concerned made this method a Christian way of doing business. That discovery took them one step beyond George Schuyler's appeal.

Presently this group held a bazaar to which everyone they knew was asked to bring his old magazines. These they sold to each other at the regular price, and the cooperative group got six dollars as their first working capital. With it they bought a small supply of canned goods, and for some time the two-foot table in the back room served as a counter for selling these goods to their friends.

After a while the group moved out into the front room and took over the tailor shop as a cooperative store. They bought supplies from local grocers who were willing to share their discount. When supplies ran out, Mr. Anthony would run around the corner to buy from a friendly Jewish grocer. So far there was no question of salaries for anybody or of rebates from this cooperative venture, which was still hardly more than a cooperative buying club. Mr. Anthony had given up his job as manager of a chain store to put full time into this work, and most of his friends were unemployed and glad to give volunteer help. They swept the store, washed the windows, kept the books, and delivered orders, all without pay. They kept going through sheer enthusiasm and a sense that the cooperative movement is somehow deeply right.

At a meeting of the Interracial Fellowship held at Pendle Hill, a Quaker school at Wallingford, Pennsylvania, Mr. Anthony was asked to speak about his cooperative store. Some of Kagawa's books were on hand, especially his writings about cooperation, stressing its deeper meaning as a way of bringing about brotherhood and peace the world over. Mr. Anthony discovered these books, which contained such words as these: "Personally, I am pouring my prayers and the reddest blood of my life into the work of carrying forward this quiet, undramatic, economic reformation. Oh, God, make haste! Teach the world's Christians the cooperative way. Set thy people in every land to the task of creating cooperatives in which thy redeeming love shall find full and free expression and realization in our day." [1]

A young white man made the same discoveries at the same meeting and promptly became a recruit to

[1] From *Christ and Japan*, by Toyohiko Kagawa. Friendship Press, New York.

the cause of cooperation. He was E. Eldredge Brewster, the son of the director of religious education in the Methodist conference in Philadelphia. He was just out of college and wondering what to do with his life. Should he work within the church or outside it? It seemed to him that the church was doing very little to improve working conditions for the average man. At this conference Mr. Brewster discovered Kagawa's pamphlet, "The Economic Foundations of Peace," and he heard a young Negro speak about the success of a cooperative venture right there in Philadelphia. Putting the two together, he decided that here was a practical method through which the church might help to build a better world. Thereupon Mr. Brewster decided to enter Drew Theological Seminary in Madison, New Jersey. Before he did so, however, he had an experience of teamwork with Lewis Anthony. First, he started a small cooperative group among the members of the National Council of Methodist Youth in Philadelphia and asked Lewis Anthony to come and tell them about his cooperative store. Later Mr. Brewster organized a small cooperative group in Norwood, Pennsylvania, his home community, with weekly deliveries from Mr. Anthony's store.

Meanwhile Mr. Anthony tried to interest the colored churches in Philadelphia in establishing local cooperatives which would be branches of a central cooperative association. He began with his own Baptist church. His pastor was sympathetic, but the church felt that the discussion of economics had no place in religion, and most of the other Negro churches felt the same way. In vain Mr. Anthony tried to show them what Kagawa means by his famous phrase, "incarnating Christ in the cooperative movement" and by his further statement that "unless we Christians move toward the cooperative idea, our Christianity is a very abstract movement." However, Mr. Anthony and Mr. Brewster kept hammering away together at the idea, and presently the Christian Youth Cooperative Association was formed in Philadelphia, with some Negro groups in its membership.

The next year Mr. Anthony's group of young Negroes joined forces with a group of adult Negroes who had been saving their money in the hope of starting a C.M.A. store. The letters stand for Colored Merchants' Association, which operates a chain of Negro retail stores organized by the National Negro Business Men's League. That was the league to which Mr. Anthony had been writing for advice when his group first organized. The upshot was that these two Negro groups joined forces under the name chosen by the adults, United Consumers Cooperative, Inc. With funds in hand they proceeded to rent a store around the corner on Woodlawn Avenue, a main thoroughfare.

Now their problems were doubled. First, the equipment had to be bought ("on time")—a weighing machine and a refrigerator, for the new stock had progressed from canned goods only to vegetables and all kinds of groceries. In the second place, the local merchants began to cut their prices to freeze out the newcomer, not because he was a colored man but because he was a competitor. Mr. Anthony could not cut prices in his turn, because that would be against the cooperative principles so carefully studied in that back room of the tailor shop. By this time his store was serving a membership list of a hundred and fifty families, and the question was: Will they stand by, or will they go elsewhere and buy cheaper? They did stand by, because they had come to understand what that particular Rochdale principle means.

So far no rebates were being paid because it was understood that profits would stay in the business until it was securely on its feet. The profits from the first store had been two thousand dollars, and nearly all of that had been invested in the new venture. Fortunately, enough was left to make a connection with the Quaker City Wholesale organization. They require a weekly deposit against which any member may draw, and Mr. Anthony always managed to make that deposit somehow.

Time and time again the little store had to stall off its creditors day by day. Mr. Anthony says that his faith in God was all he had to go on, but it was enough. Every time he seemed to have reached the very end, something turned up. One day when he was without a cent to pay his bills, two friends dropped in and lent him the money that saved the store. Practically all of his help was volunteer help, and he himself received no salary. Often he slept behind the counter to save room rent. Like Kagawa, he took out nothing more than bare expenses for himself, and sometimes this amounted to no more than two dollars a month for laundry. Now and again his helpers in the store would take time off to get odd jobs in order to buy a suit of clothes or a pair of shoes. One summer in order to keep the store going Mr. Anthony took on a second job as time keeper, but he managed to run the store just the same.

The weekly turnover was now nearly one hundred dollars.

Along with opposition to the new venture there were new friends, too. One of them was a Negro dentist, Dr. Howard, with too much time on his hands because his practice had suffered during the depression. He was the only member of the group who had a car, and he put it at the disposal of the cooperative store.

In 1935 the store moved again, following the direction of its membership to a more densely populated neighborhood on Fairmount Avenue. Here there was less opposition, because by this time Mr. Anthony was well known and well liked, and also because people had come to understand that he was not trying to force other stores to the wall. His store still depended somewhat on volunteer service, but it was a going concern, with over four hundred and sixty families on its membership list from several districts of Philadelphia. Its annual business was over five thousand dollars and it employed fifteen clerks.

When the Division of Self-Help Cooperatives of the FERA was organized, Mr. Anthony applied for a government grant. At this point the experience which had already enlisted Jewish and Methodist help became international and picked up a Finnish cooperator. He was Frank Aaltonen, formerly the manager of the United Farmers Cooperative of Fitchburg, Massachusetts. He had met Mr. Anthony at the Cooperative Congress held in New York City in 1932. Mr. Anthony had hitch-hiked to the meeting, rather than take money out of the store to pay railroad or bus fare. When the reports of various cooperatives were being given, Mr. Anthony told the story of the struggle of the United Consumers Cooperative, Inc. Mr. Aaltonen, who was present as a delegate from the Fitchburg cooperative, remembered that story three years later when he was connected with the Division of Self-Help Cooperatives of the FERA. When Mr. Anthony's application came in he recalled the man who wouldn't take money out of the cooperative store for his transportation, and had the application approved. On it were the signatures of many responsible citizens of Philadelphia who were willing to give proof of faith in Mr. Anthony. "He has friends all over the city who were glad to sign," says Eldredge Brewster. "My father signed first." There were friends in that interracial fellowship, friends among Philadelphia lawyers and ministers, both colored and white, as well as friends in the Eastern States Cooperative League, of which Mr. Anthony's group was now a member. This readiness to sign was a visible proof that Kagawa is right when he insists that consumers' cooperation will bring all sorts of people together.

The FERA grant was six thousand dollars. It is being used to run a farm in Georgetown, Pennsylvania, to supply vegetables for the cooperative store. The farm itself was offered without rent by a white woman in New York City who had somehow heard of this cooperative. The expense came in buying farm equipment and fixing up residence quarters. Out of the thousands of Negroes on relief, Mr. Anthony picked five families who had had experience in farming. Each family was allotted a plot for its own use and they all worked together on the part that belonged to the store. This was another leaf out of Kagawa's notebook, for he has often suggested that rural congregations work together to raise one crop for the church.

A staff member of the Cooperative League of the U.S.A. has visited this United Consumers Cooperative, Inc. This is his comment: "This shows what cooperation can do even in a rock-bottom situation. When Negroes succeed in anything like that, you can be sure that they have had to work twice as hard as whites. Maybe, if you are willing to work, there is some advantage in starting from a backward situation, as this Negro group had to do, because you can skip some of the stages in development as you come forward. That's what Japan did; it learned by other people's mistakes and avoided them. I think this cooperative forged ahead something like that. It had a strong leader who insisted upon study, and he attracted a group who threw themselves into it with religious devotion." Mark the last two words, for they give the point of the story.

What had happened to the original Young Negroes' Cooperative League in the meantime? It had got off to a good start with two national conferences, one in 1931 and the second—and last—in 1932. Groups had been formed all over the country, but their motive of winning power for the race did not prove strong enough to carry through the depression. Once more Kagawa had been proved right; only "the love motive," to use his term, is able to supply enough energy to create the spirit of sacrifice necessary to keep this kind of venture going.

The United Consumers Cooperative has come a long way from the point where it shared the league's interest in gaining power for Negroes. Now it joins hands with other young people, both colored and white, through the Christian Youth Cooperative Association of Philadelphia. Through the Cooperative League of the U.S.A. it feels itself a part of the movement in the whole country. What is more, through knowing Kagawa it has come to see what he saw long ago: that "the cooperative movement offers the church a technique of brotherhood," a definite method of building a better world. No wonder that the group has grown to fit the job.

"Why, I could name half a dozen boys in that original group," says Eldredge Brewster, "whose whole personalities have been literally made by this experience. They are young men that anybody would be glad to know." The reason seems to be that they are happy to have found a practical way of expressing their Christianity. Their happiness looks like a proof of one more of Kagawa's statements: "This cooperative movement, rooted as it is in love and brotherhood, is unquestionably an out-and-out Christian movement."

SIX

THEY had graduated from the eighth grade, and that was as far as the six-months-a-year school for colored children went in their little Virginia town. Half a dozen of them, though, were desperately eager to go on to high school, and one or two were even planning to work their way through college. They knew the desired port, but there was no gangplank to the only ship. So these boys and girls besieged their teachers, begging them for lessons out of school hours. They would study hard, they promised. And the teachers couldn't refuse. For two years they gave their time—until the parents gradually had managed to make other arrangements.

One of these children was Mary Elizabeth Branch, now one of the two Negro women who are college presidents.

Mary Branch's home was the kind of home that makes a boy or girl want to get ahead, and so all six of the children went off to work their way through college or normal school. When Mary Branch was born her race was ninety-five per cent unlettered, but she started far ahead of the rank and file because both her parents, though without schooling, were intelligent and could read and write. Her father was a shoemaker, one of those men of whom Booker T. Washington wrote in 1906, in his autobiography, *Up from Slavery:* "If one goes today into any Southern town and asks for the leading and most reliable colored men in the community, I believe that in five cases out of ten he would be directed to a Negro who learned a trade in the days of slavery."

Whatever these parents knew, they shared eagerly with their children, for they realized that Negro children would have to go fast and far. "My parents came out of slavery with only their bare hands," is how Miss Branch tells the story nowadays. "I have yet to see my father's superior as a shoemaker. Of course all his work was done by hand. . . . Daily we were instructed to make the most of our lives. We were trained not only to read good books but to take our turn day by day in reading them aloud to father, mother and the smaller children. We interpreted what we read, or listened to the interpretation from mother, father, or sisters and brothers.

Father read aloud each night for an hour or more from newspapers, magazines or books. He subscribed to three newspapers and he was well informed on all kinds of topics. He knew the facts of history and could interpret them better than many a college graduate. He accumulated a fair collection of good books—religious, biographical, historical and philosophical. In fact, he read the best literature, both poetry and prose. One would easily have taken him for a college graduate. So you see I grew up in an atmosphere of intellectual strivings." No wonder that all six of the children worked their way through college or normal school.

Such parents were naturally among the leading colored citizens of Farmville, Virginia, where Mary Branch grew up. Farmville is a pretty little college town in which the life of the white community centers around the State College for white girls. Her home, she says modestly, "was the second-best Negro home in the town." A friend pictures it as spacious, set back from the street on a well kept lawn with two old magnolia trees still blooming. The Branch family worked harder than any of their neighbors and always thought of themselves as poor, but they found time to care for the lawn and the roses. What little extra money they had went to the African Methodist Episcopal Church and for educating the children.

Out of this background Tazewell Branch, less than ten years out of slavery, was elected to the legislature of Virginia for two terms of two years each. In those Reconstruction Days, the Republican party was promoting the idea, later abandoned, of Negro political action. Following his service in the legislature he became collector of internal revenue for four years. "These honors were literally forced upon him," writes his daughter, "by his friends, black and white, who respected him highly for his intelligence, integrity, unusual common sense, and good judgment."

Unfortunately, after those terms of public office it became harder for the Branch family to make a living. The father was growing old, and, besides, as machinery began to come in a hand-worker became a "back number." From now on the mother carried the major load of educating the six children. "My mother was a doer," Miss Branch says. She would can, dry, preserve and pickle fruits and vegetables, in addition to working on the outside. She managed to keep her children fed, and she gave them the example of unbeatable courage. It was a fine bringing-up for Mary Branch, who as a Negro college president would also have to make bricks without straw.

Mary Branch was thirteen when she began to "attend" the State College in Farmville. Not that she was admitted into a college for white girls, for such admission would not be legal in Virginia. But, as she says, "I did attend the State College in Farmville, for my mother washed clothes for a number of girls and teachers, and I attended regularly to get clothes or to take them. I also helped to clean in the institution and maneuvered to be one of those assigned to clean the library. I always thrilled when I entered it, though I never dared stop and read any of the books. I enjoyed reading the titles and glancing at the tables of contents.

"However, that small library of not more than from five to six thousand books inspired me. I made up my mind that I would some day have the advantage of a good library in a good college. This inspiration stayed with me. I had visions during my waking hours and dreams during my sleeping hours of being a student in the state college there at home. How the white girls would stare at me! But I would read right on in that library."

89

Sleeping and waking dreams are likely to become facts, especially when the dreamer has a sturdy body and more brains than the average. Mary Branch was one of those eighth-grade graduates mentioned early in the story who begged so hard for more schooling that they got it. Afterward she went off to finish her high school course in Petersburg, Virginia, where a newly established land-grant college for Negroes had a high school department. Here she finished the high school and the normal course. The present dean of women says of her: "The round-faced, bright-eyed, intelligent-looking girl even then gave promise of an unusual life. She was alert and precocious as a student, graduating at an early age with honors."

The year after graduation found Miss Branch teaching in an elementary school at Blackstone, Virginia, for $27.50 a month. At that time teaching was the only avenue open to an educated Negro woman, but even if she could have entered any profession in the world, teaching was what she would have chosen. The job matched the person. Before long her own college called her back to teach English, and there she stayed for several years.

There is always one person in every group to whom everybody turns, and Miss Branch has always been that person. The moment she steps into the room her personality, at once strong and pleasing, begins to take effect. Students like her voice, with its firm but mellow tone of one who knows what she is talking about. They like her well groomed look and have a sense of being with a woman so sure of herself that she can help them.

In no time "Branch's English" became the most popular course on the campus, not because it was a snap course but because it was the hardest and most interesting. How she made the boys and girls work, and how they loved to work under her direction! She was one of those who are sure to put joy in the classroom first and keep details from becoming drudgery. Other English teachers sought her out to ask: "What does this passage mean? How can I teach it so as to mean the most to our students? You know them so much better than I do." And that was true, for Miss Branch had been the house director for the boys' dormitory and later for the girls' dormitory. The boys sought her out to talk with her about their favorite girls, and the girls came to talk about the boys. Moreover, many problems of discipline or management landed at Miss Branch's door because she knew how to listen to both sides, and she has the kind of strength that makes other people stronger.

During these years at Petersburg Miss Branch had been doing systematic reading, taking extension courses, and going off to summer school. Presently she went to the University of Chicago and earned the degree of Bachelor of Philosophy, and later the Master's degree. Afterward she became the dean of women at Vashon Girls' High School in St. Louis. This was at the time the largest high school for Negro girls in the country, and thus Mary Branch had arrived, professionally speaking, at the highest point in teaching in secondary schools. The salary was good, and she found the work easy because she enjoyed it, though the school was in the poorest Negro neighborhood. But, as Miss Branch says, "I've always had a missionary streak, a deep sympathy for the more underprivileged of my race. I visited homes in all kinds of shacks under almost frightening conditions. Several parents said I was the first teacher who had ever visited them." Because of her excellent record, the school board transferred her to a better-paying position in the normal school, but she asked to be transferred back.

Out of a clear sky came a call from the American Missionary Association to become the president of

Tillotson College in Austin, Texas. Through a desperate combination of circumstances it had run so far down that it was all but off the map. The American Missionary Association might, in a different case, have decided that by this time the local public schools were adequate for colored children, and so might have closed the school; but they felt that a Christian institution was needed at this particular spot, although they realized that it must become a better school, one that would be accredited by the state. A strong leader would be needed, and they looked for her in the field of public school education. A woman markedly successful, with strong Christian qualities —whom should they choose?

Miss Branch was exactly the person anyway they looked at her, and they called her. Twice she refused point-blank. Going would mean not only giving up the best salary she had ever received, but also turning down the offer of a city college position where with summer work she could make twice what the American Missionary Association could pay her at Tillotson. The American Missionary Association persisted. Then, says Miss Branch, "I thought of the numbers of white teachers who had gone South for years since the Civil War and worked among an alien

race for no other reason than a Christian interest in
the underprivileged. They had made far greater sac-
rifices than I would be called upon to make. I thought
and prayed over the matter and finally got a definite
feeling that I should go to Tillotson. I have not yet
regretted my choice."

Miss Branch didn't take the next train home after
her first view of the Tillotson College campus, and
this proved that she had courage. She had known
that her job was to save a dying college, but on first
sight she thought it already dead. One has to remember that she saw it through eyes familiar with the
green lawns of two northern universities.

Tillotson College is built on a thirteen-acre knoll
within the small capital city of Texas. On the first
of July, 1930, Miss Branch entered the campus
through the wretched remains of a fence and proceeded up a gullied and scraggly path through
underbrush so thick that a fox could—and did—hide
in it. Thorny old mesquite trees, rotted by storms,
sagged all over the hill. Among them were half a
dozen buildings, one of which had been built in 1881
as the first Negro collegiate building west of the
Mississippi and looked its age. On an opposite hill
stood a two-story contraption covered with tarred

paper; this turned out to be the laundry. Miss Branch proceeded up the wooden steps and across the uneven floors of the dormitory. She next visited the administration building, in which a room eight by ten feet proved to be the president's office. Here another woman might have sat down and cried; this one sat down to plan. As another Tillotson professor says of her, "You just can't tell Mary Branch that something can't be done, for she begins to plan right away how it can be done." The American Missionary Association had no money in the budget, but they gave her a free hand. The story of what happened proves that she was one who could make bricks without straw.

So Miss Branch began to mother a forlorn college back to life and health. Where does one begin in a situation where everything needs to be done at once? At least Miss Branch had a free hand and nine new professors with good training. She began to depend on them. If she knew what they thought about working under a woman president, she gave no sign. The first thing they all did together was to make a general survey in order to develop a five-year plan. When they knew where they were—it was plain to see where they were not—then they could move ahead on all fronts at once. With Mary Branch, as might be guessed, the library came first. She had passed it on her way to the office and noted its three thousand dilapidated volumes. Once these were sorted out, less than half of them proved to be fit for college reference work. What kind of books were needed most? The state education law settled that point, for in Texas every college student must earn one-fifth of all his credits in the subject of education. But how could books be bought with a tiny budget that was needed in a dozen directions at once? Miss Branch wrote to hundreds of her friends for books. She besieged the second-hand bookstores of Austin which handle the books from five local colleges and universities. From that time on every college department was to take its annual turn in receiving new books. Thus the library was brought steadily forward to the goal of the twelve thousand volumes required by the Southern Association of Schools and Colleges as a minimum for the coveted A rating.

Of those forlorn buildings, which one should first be renewed? Miss Branch decided to begin with the laundry. So that ancient eye-sore was promptly torn down and a new laundry was built behind the girls' dormitory. Then came the turn of the old industrial building. It was cleaned out, painted, and rearranged.

New equipment was bought somehow; it was small, but adequate. There were a few sewing machines, stoves, a refrigerator, and pipes for gas. "We do our best to make our girls scientifically domestic," said Miss Branch, "because that helps them both to get a job and keep a husband." Next came the turn of the girls' dormitory. Most of its furniture went to the junk heap, new floors were laid, and new conveniences added to attract girls from decent homes.

That historic fox had long since been scared away. A crew of men from Austin had cleared away the tangles of grass, cut down the worst of the mesquite trees, and planted young sycamores, elms, and chinaberries. The clearing opened the way for a carpet of blue-bonnets, those hardy Texas wild flowers. The paths were graveled and the borders planted with roses.

The uppermost problem now was, "How to get better students to match a better plant?" Another campaign was mapped out. To be sure, a campus chock full of beginnings would be likely to attract intelligent students, but the college also began to reach out through the state with letters and speeches. Soon the old high school department was dropped, thereby doubling the college budget. Then a plan of

97

student self-help was worked out through which ninety per cent of the students could earn part of their way instead of having to leave college every other year to earn a hundred and eighty dollars for annual fees. As the standard went steadily up, better students began to be attracted. Some of the professors made tennis courts and laid out a baseball diamond and an outdoor basketball court, while others started the students on the road to intercollegiate debating. At last accounts Tillotson College had two teams in a triangular intercollegiate debate, and both teams won.

Better students with a higher grade of college life proceeded to push the old chapel exercises far out of date. Formerly chapel had been compulsory and of the sermon variety hated by the students. Now it was made voluntary during the week, and the professors put their wits together to discover the sort of programs that students would attend. A combination of faculty and student leadership soon proved the most acceptable. For example, the students in education might present a debate or students in English might present a dramatic sketch. Later a college pastor was found, a graduate from the Oberlin School of Religion who knows how to encourage the whole religious life of the campus. Miss Branch herself, by the way, had joined the Episcopal church at Petersburg because there was no A.M.E. Church in that college town. Later in Austin for the same reason she joined the Congregational-Christian fellowship. Her father had "always said he didn't care what church his children went to so long as they went to work in it."

Soon the whole faculty of Tillotson College had to be improved to keep up with the better grade of students. Before 1930 only one professor had a Master's degree. All the new instructors had that much, but not one had a Ph.D. By now every professor understands that getting this higher degree through further study is his goal. From the beginning such a goal was part of that five-year plan. "Oh, yes," says one of the professors, "we knew right away that Tillotson just had to become a Grade A college in time. That rating depends partly on our degrees. Our girls' college won the B rating in 1933. Now we are growing a crop of boys to match the girls. Our first one has just received his diploma. We haven't dormitory room for boys on the campus; therefore they have to come in as day students."

Every afternoon between two and half-past four,

99

Tillotson College welcomes visitors, and student guides are on hand to show off their college. They may take a guest to see a home economics exhibit, or the collection of maps and charts and items of historic interest in the education museum, or one of a dozen other sights. The air is full of the thrill of something being done. A visitor may ask: "But how did you get the money to do all this?"

The answer may be: "Our president knows how to make a very little go a very long way." If the visitor asks something more about Miss Branch, any student can tell him that she has received two honorary degrees, the degree of LL.D. from Howard University, and the first degree of Doctor of Pedagogy given by Virginia State College for Negroes. The student is sure to add that Miss Branch is the only Negro woman in the country who is president of a senior college accredited by the Southern Association of Schools and Colleges. But words are likely to fail a student when he tries to describe her combination of energy, tolerance, good humor, and persistence, and he is likely to end:

"Why, she's just our Miss Branch."

SEVEN

A HOME-MADE SCHOOL IN THE DEEP SOUTH

TOBY was only a farm mule, but his death meant a crisis for a whole colored school. A few days after his death it took three members of the school staff to open the mail containing letters of regret and one dollar bills to help toward the purchase of a new Toby. Only a mule, mind you! But firmly attached to the mule was a boy whose only way of keeping in school was to take care of Toby, and besides that boy were five or six hundred other boys and girls whose whole chance of schooling was involved in the farm on which Toby had been working. Without Toby, how could the school crops be cultivated and what would the students have to eat? And how could the boys stay in school unless they had vegetables to sell to the kitchen department?

In other words, so delicately balanced were the workings of the school that the loss of Toby would mean the loss of a student. Therefore, the principal set the story in type and struck off a letter of appeal on his hand press.

"We pitched a crop," he had written, "counting on Toby to help cultivate and harvest it. His death has thrown us back a good deal. To catch up and also to harvest all the hay we can, we ought to have a pair of mules. This would also mean that two boys could work their way in school."

What school is this where the balance of work and study is so closely calculated that "minus one mule" means "minus one boy"? Not Tuskegee, for that institute is long past the stage where farm work proceeds by mule power, and it is too heavily endowed to be staggered by the loss of one farm animal. Also many years have passed since Tuskegee was a one-man institution, dependent on Booker T. Washington to raise funds through friendships.

True, this small farm school which lost Toby is a sort of Tuskegee of the early days. Imagine the dense pine woods of a state in the deep South, flavor the air with the scent of old pines and of rough pine lumber, listen for bird-calls and the ringing of tools all day long, and you have the setting of the Piney Woods Country Life School in Mississippi. So thick are the woods that the school can hardly be seen from a hill a mile away. Even more completely hidden in the woods of the surrounding forest counties are nests of log cabins, many of which were built by slaves before the Civil War and are today inhabited by their descendants, practically slaves themselves under the sharecropping system of tenantry.

Before this school was started, thousands of Negroes in this area were living half-animal lives, hidden away from all outside help. More than a third of them were unable to read or write or figure their own rentals. During the course of a year they would handle little or no money. And it was among these people that this school started, under a cedar tree, with no backing whatever. The founder was literally betting his life that the rural Negro was worth educating.

Laurence Clifton Jones, founder and principal of this school, has been telling its story for more than twenty-five years. Hundreds of audiences in the Middle West have heard him tell how the school has grown literally "from the woods and friends." Continuing chapters come from the hand printing press every time somethings happens—like the death of Toby. The first question which Mr. Jones is asked after he has finished a speech telling the story of the school is likely to be: "But why did you choose to go back to the South, into the hardest possible situation?" Mr. Jones is always willing to tell his own story in reply.

His father was a hotel porter in St. Joseph, Missouri, a town where a colored boy was welcome to attend the white high school and use the public library. Laurence Jones went to Marshalltown, Iowa, to complete his high school course and here he made his expenses by work in restaurants and hotels. He was the first colored graduate of the school, and the audience cheered when he received his diploma in 1903. He went on to work his way through Iowa State University, where he graduated with honors in 1907. While there he heard the famous tale of Mark Hopkins—that Mark Hopkins at one end of a log and a boy at the other would make a university by themselves! Then he discovered that Mark Hopkins had been the teacher of General Armstrong, who had in his turn founded Hampton Institute and taught Booker T. Washington. Thereupon this student began to read everything he could find about the founder of Tuskegee Institute. From that moment, though the two men were never to meet, Booker T. Washington began to teach Laurence

Clifton Jones what an educated Negro can and should do to bring forward the less fortunate members of his race.

After graduation from the university, Laurence Jones was invited to join the staff at Tuskegee Institute, but he chose to go to one of the many struggling offshoots of the famous school. This one was located in Hinds County, Mississippi. It paid him less than five hundred dollars for two years of teaching, but it gave him the chance to learn what the Mississippi Negro was like and why. He knew by this time their general reputation as "no-count 'n' lazy," and he knew that every other man in Mississippi was a black man. He had learned that the black half of the population, by and large, had made almost no progress since the Civil War, but he did not know why this was so. Now he set out to explore the poorer hill counties where some of his pupils lived.

For six months he visited around, traveling by mule or ox wagon or walking fifteen miles a day, and lighting his way through the great dark woods with a pine torch at night. He slept on the dirt floor of cabins built for slaves of half a century ago; he ate coarse cornmeal with the stringy meat of razor-back hogs. And all the time he talked about modern farm methods to men who had never heard of them. To most of these people he was the only man they knew who could read and write, except possibly some preacher, and they began calling him "Fesser," shortened from "Professor." He found them anxious to educate their children, but with no possible way of doing it. They owned nothing but the ragged clothes they wore and a few primitive tools and household utensils.

These Negroes were sharecroppers, growing and picking some white owner's cotton supposedly for half a share in the profits, but in reality getting hardly a penny from one year's end to the next. How could they know the market price of cotton and consequently what their share should be? How could they tell that the plantation store was often making a hundred per cent profit on its sales to them, when a white agent kept the books which none of them could read? What could they say when the agent assured them that they were in his debt because their year's labor had not covered their supplies of food and clothing? No wonder that most of them had lost all ambition—why not be lazy when there was no hope of ever making more than the barest living? "Fesser" Jones, though, thought that he knew the cure for that kind of laziness, and he set about raising money for a school building.

One local Negro group had been saving money for fifteen years in order to start a school, but they could not persuade themselves to trust their few precious dollars to "Fesser" Jones because he was a "furriner." Mr. Jones finally remembered Mark Hopkins. He decided to quit working for a building and look around for a log. Pine logs were plentiful, and so the news was passed around that school was about to open. Three boys occupied the first log under a cedar tree one October morning in 1910. The number soon grew to twenty-nine, and two students from Mr. Jones's first school came down to help with the teaching. November came on chilly, and the three classes had to gather about three bonfires. No shelter was near except an ancient two-room log cabin, once a slave dwelling and now tenanted by snakes, owls, lizards and an occasional flock of sheep. Mr. Jones persuaded the owner to donate the "sheep cuddy," along with forty acres of land and fifty dollars in cash. Thereupon the school joyfully adjourned to the wreck to see what could be done with it. The lizards and other occupants were dispossessed. New "classes" went into action. The "carpentry class" laid a flooring, repaired the sagging walls and roof, put a dirt-and-stick chimney at either end, and made benches. The "painting class" cut down the weeds and then white-washed the walls, inside and out.

Soon the teaching staff was able to take up its quarters in the smaller room. The larger space suddenly became seven rooms in one: chapel first of all, then office, recitation room, study hall, carpenter shop, sewing-room and basket-making establishment. Land was cleared, a farm was started, a bit of school money was secured from the county, with small but regular donations of cash and labor and eggs and potatoes from the now interested neighbors. The school closed its first year out of debt and with eighty-five students. Some of them stayed on that summer to raise a crop with their bare hands, for as yet there was not even one "Toby."

The next year the school went ahead on sheer faith, with five teachers and one hundred students. There was also one extension worker paid by the newly established Jeanes Fund, for Mr. Jones saw from the very start that the school could never get ahead faster than its community. On a hand press given by a friend, the school began to print a midget newspaper, *The Pine Torch*. The present schedule of alternate work and study began out of sheer necessity, for the boys had to work half a day to keep the school farm going, and the girls had to work to keep the students fed and housed.

In another year, local interest had been so stirred by this plucky venture that the white people of Braxton, the nearest town, gave the money for a dormitory which would house forty girls. The boys proceeded to build it from the rough pine logs at hand, and their economy of material was such that three more buildings were managed "from the scraps"—a log cabin for blacksmithing and broom-making, another for manual training, and a barn where the boys might live. "Fesser" Jones and his new bride got the original cabin as a wedding present for their own quarters. Mrs. Jones used it from the first as a demonstration center in home-making. Whatever she did to make her home attractive at small cost, she did before the eyes of fascinated neighbors. She continued to do this and also to take charge of women's industries with both charm and efficiency until her recent death.

When the school was five years old it applied for a charter, and the president of Braxton Bank was one of several white men who signed the petition. The school was officially known from that time on as the Piney Woods Country Life School. Mr. Jones says he still thinks that the most important article in the charter was the pledge "to keep the cost of education at the lowest possible point consistent with efficient operation, and so to bring education within the ability of the poor classes of the Black Belt."

Ever since those days the school has kept "inchin' along," in the words of a favorite spiritual, until now eight hundred people, students and staff, are housed on a farm campus of twelve hundred acres. It is a self-contained community with its own electric light plant, a hundred-thousand-gallon water tower of steel to supply its own water system, and its own post-office, named Piney Woods, Mississippi. It has a community house, too, with rooms for the guests who come almost every day to visit the campus.

The visitors are people from far and near who have an interest in education for country life. They enter through an attractive archway and drive along an excellent road, forewarned that everything they see, including the roads and drives, is home-made. Most of them have come on purpose to learn how something can be made out of nothing under primitive conditions. If they are from the tropics—and many of them are—they find something familiar in the long grey moss hanging from the live-oaks, in the darkness of the thick woods on every side, and in those long luxuriant pine needles. "It all has a far-off look of the jungle," commented a woman who had gone to Africa also to observe rural education.

The visitors include both white and colored people. An official of the state department of education comes regularly and the best white people of the state are friendly to the school. The principal of the white high school at Braxton brings his seniors over on an annual trip. Thomas Campbell often swings around from Tuskegee Institute. Mississippi is one of the seven Gulf states for which he is field agent, and he comes over to confer with the Smith-Hughes vocational worker who lives on the campus, or with one of the home extension workers. A visiting British commissioner of education from South Africa studies those things that colored children of farmers in Cape Province or the Transvaal could profitably learn about—the chicken houses and the dairy barn, the sweet potato drying house and the broom-making and cobbling shops. But he will probably think that the garages and auto repair shops are too modern to be of use to most of them at present. A visiting professor of education from a Northern university is most keenly interested in the fact that what was originally planned for a high school has developed at both ends. It has grown forward to include the first two years of an industrial junior college. At the lower end a Rosenwald Training School has been added which takes the neighboring children through the first six grades, and at the same time provides teacher training for students. The word "neighboring" signifies a wide area when used to describe the children who attend this school, for some of them walk as much as twelve miles a day in order to do so.

Visitors are usually taken past the new cement academic building to see the original log cabin which was the school's first house. It has been roofed over by a recent graduating class in order to preserve it. After that the visitors may wander around at will or ask to be shown over the campus. Any student will tell them the story of the disastrous fires that overtook the first rough frame dormitories but were re-sponsible for the present buildings of brick and cement. Many of the boys and girls will tell how, not so long ago, they each came walking in from the deep woods with all their possessions tied up in a red bandanna handkerchief. It was a boy who wrote the following letter to Mr. Jones, but many a girl has written him one like it:

"You say for me Bring $10.00 to entrance and $6.50 for books. I Dont see no way I can get that. But I can get them now if it is eney way that you can give me something to do. I would like the best in the worl to go to school, if you can give me a job that I can work my way compleat throue. I can Do som of most every kind of work." [1]

Mr. Jones would probably reply: "Come along anyhow." A new boy would then be set to raise the corn, sorghum, black-eyed peas and sweet potatoes for the school. He would be learning scientific farming under the direction of the state department of agriculture, and he would sell the product to the school kitchen, pay his bills of eight dollars a month and have a bit left over. In the trade shops he would find his own level, somewhere between shoe-mending and auto repair work. He would learn arithmetic by weighing the cost and profits of a cow against the cost and profits of raising cotton. His chemistry might be learned through the making of molasses, and his geometry through carpentry.

[1] From *The Pine Torch*, September, 1933. By permission.

To be sure, it would be a tremendous task for a boy from the average rural school to get all these principles into his head, even if he could have all his time to do it. One geometry teacher gives a student's explanation of why he was making slow progress. Five other boys had made room for him in their living quarters. There they were studying in relays all night, one pair working for two hours at a time by a kerosene lamp.

It is such boys as these who go out to convince desperate farmers that a Negro can pull himself out of the muck. It is no accident that farmers within reach of Piney Woods have bought six thousand acres of land within the last ten years—more than they had bought in the twenty years previous. Graduates of the school, to be sure, cannot take all the credit, for every teacher expects to do some extension work during vacations. Thus the number of persons reached by the school in many ways is never less than ten thousand a year.

What if the entering student is a girl? She might have to sleep "four in a bed," but she has a chance to learn a dozen ways of making a living and helping a community. She learns not only laundering but how to cook those famous four-cent meals. She also learns sewing, and how to care for a garden and poultry. She may learn how to make baskets of the long pine needles that can be worked into patterns like stiff lace. Or there is the Rosenwald Training School if she is willing to take the hardest job of all. Many of these graduates plan to go into rural teaching in a state which spends one nickel for a colored child's education to every nine nickels spent for the white child's. The schoolhouse is likely to be a tumbledown one, unpainted, with no windows and no blackboards, and the pay about twenty dollars a month for a three- or four-month term. A girl who goes to such a school expects to be a little Piney Woods all by herself, slowly raising the level of the whole community as the Country Life School has gradually raised the rural Negro's level of living in all the surrounding counties.

No trip to the school would be complete without hearing the students sing spirituals in the old-fashioned way, with none of the quirks of melody ironed out. They even compose spirituals, for they are still living fairly close to the primitive conditions under which the first ones were spontaneously thrown together. The school has four quartets, known as the Cotton Blossom Singers, on the road the year round,

making friends for the school wherever their concerts are given.

By running under sacrificial steam all these years,
the Piney Woods Country Life School has been able
to reach the long-neglected rural Negro of the deep
South. He was so far down that it took a special effort to get down to where he was, and its founder
was among the pioneers with the faith and courage to
do that. At the end of twenty-five years Laurence
Clifton Jones says: "Only since I opened the Piney
Woods School have I really begun to live."

EIGHT

YOUNG NEGRO LEADERS OF AMERICANS

I. Martin L. Harvey

MOST boys and girls know something about the Christian Youth Council of North America, but not all of them know that the president from 1934 to 1936 was a young Negro, Martin Luther Harvey. He was elected on the conference grounds at Lake Geneva, Wisconsin, by the hundred-odd young men and women from all the denominations represented in the council. A scant half-dozen of the delegates were Negroes, and so it must have been a white majority that elected Mr. Harvey. Who is he, and how did it happen?

It was the Y.M.C.A. that gave Martin Harvey his first chance for leadership. When he was in high school in Hempstead, N. Y., one of several Negro students in a class of four hundred, the colored secretary of the Nassau-Suffolk County Y.M.C.A. of Long Island discovered him. The boy was the son of the pastor of the A.M.E. Zion Church, the largest local colored church at that time, and hence a man of influence. The Negro community of Hempstead, dating from the time of the American Revolution, had numbered less than two hundred in a population of twenty thousand people until the ranks were suddenly swollen by the migrations from the South after the World War. From out of the older and more privileged group the secretaries of the county Y.M. C.A. were hoping to develop leaders who could help with the new community problem. With this in mind they began to watch Martin Harvey. At that time they were selecting a junior board from members of the churches in the county, and the Negro Y.M.C.A. secretary nominated Martin Harvey. He thus became the only colored member of the board among a score of white boys, most of whom he had not met before. They liked him on acquaintance and chose him as vice president of the board.

The next year the president of the board resigned because he was going away to college. Should the vice president be promoted to fill the place? Discussion raged among the boys. It was as though they looked at Martin for the first time and saw his color as a barrier. The Y.M.C.A. staff kept its hands off the decision, but the white secretary pointed out the real issues at stake. They were not so simple, he said, as the one question: "Shall we have a colored boy for president?" The most important question was: "Would Martin Harvey do a good job?" Next, "Are you willing to elect a president who cannot be taken into many of your homes or asked to your social affairs? If you are, all right. But stop and think now, and be sure what you're doing." Some years later the Y.M.C.A. secretaries painstakingly pointed out the same issues to a larger group when Martin was being considered for president of the New York State Youth Council. In both cases Martin was elected.

Still hoping to develop a future leader for his race, the Y.M.C.A. secretaries presently picked Martin Harvey as the first Negro delegate from his county to the New York State Youth Council. He proved to be undismayed at finding himself the only Negro among six hundred white young people. In fact, what he did there led directly to his being sent to the Older Boys' and Girls' Leadership Conference held every summer at Lake Winnepesaukee, New Hampshire. Martin had this training for three summers, and usually he was the only colored boy among fifty or more. By this time, and not entirely through his own choice and effort, he was set on the path which he has followed ever since. That is the difficult path of the rare Negro whose work lies more among whites than it does among his own race. His friends in the Y.M.C.A. may have wondered where such a path would lead, but they kept on backing him.

One of the program advisers of the Nassau-Suffolk County Y.M.C.A. was Dr. Samuel L. Hamilton, head of the Department of Religious Education of New York University. Martin's father, an exceptionally well equipped Negro minister, had a college degree, and it seemed natural for Martin to enter New York University. His major was religious education. As his course went on, he chose to carry increasing outside responsibilities. On Long Island he was helping that junior board of the Y.M.C.A. in a new and exciting program. They were organizing one commission after another to consider such tremendous topics as war and peace, vocational guidance, and international relations. These commissions usually turned into forum teams that went from place to place conducting discussions among the young people of the churches, mostly white.

By this time Martin Harvey had been chosen as president of the New York State Youth Council.

His own denomination claimed him in his junior year at college and made him its Youth Secretary for the Department of Christian Education. Now he had to organize church conferences and provide monthly copy for the young people's magazine. How could he find time for the less thrilling job of study? He did not fail to get his degree, but he cut his commencement exercises because he was due at Knoxville, Tennessee, for the General Church School Convention of the A.M.E. Zion Church. From here he went directly north to attend the third session of the Christian Youth Council of North America, meeting at Lake Geneva, Wisconsin, in June, 1934.

This Christian Youth Council had been launched in 1926 by the International Council of Religious Education. At the second meeting in 1930 a permanent method of selecting delegates was worked out. Thus in 1934 four young people with one adult adviser were chosen from each state or province from the denominations, the Y.M.C.A. and the Y.W.C.A., the International Society of Christian Endeavor, and other young people's organizations. Only one Negro denomination was sufficiently in touch with the Council to send delegates, and that was Martin Harvey's, the African Methodist Episcopal Zion Church. One hundred and thirteen young men and women arrived at Lake Geneva with their advisers and several additional resource leaders. Martin Harvey found himself literally twice a delegate. Representing his denomination he was the adult adviser, with a delegation of four, but he was also youth delegate from the New York State Youth Council. His speech on the opening night aroused the enthusiasm of the conference when he said, in effect, "Let's not talk about our beliefs, but let's do something about them."

However, the delegates were immediately divided into six commissions for a week of discussion to precede action. What were the main subjects selected? This was the list: Youth's Statement of Faith and Philosophy; Working for Peace; Building a Christian Economic Order; Facing the Liquor Problem; Extending Friendship among the Races; and last of all, Developing a Program of Action. Where would Mr. Harvey be of the greatest use as a discussion leader? Almost any white group would be likely to assign him to the commission on race, though as a matter of fact, he would have preferred to join either the commission on peace or the one on economics. It is often true that colored leaders would rather discuss something else than race, but their

122

white friends are likely to drag them back to the very topic that has the most painful memories. So Mr. Harvey was not surprised when he found himself the assistant discussion leader with the group that was working on race questions. Perhaps it was just as well, for, as he says:

"Of course the race problem is my major interest. However, it is often better to approach it from some other angle, such as peace. It's a question of technique, but in this case we really could talk straight with each other."

As a result of drawing on first-hand experience, the report of his commission drives home the difficulties that a typical colored boy or girl may meet among Christian groups. A white boy can learn a lot about what happens to a Negro boy just by reading some of the recommendations for improvement:

Put conference delegates in the homes of other races instead of putting them off by themselves.
Include members of other races in all Christian conferences and camps, with interracial housing.
Plan for interracial cooperation in civic activities, in dramatics and recreation.

Protest to teachers and principals who allow the ridicule or belittling of other races in the public schools.

The result of six days of acquaintance was that Martin L. Harvey was elected by his mates there on the conference grounds as President of the Christian Youth Council of North America. The choice was due to several factors. Mr. Harvey was already known to most of the delegates from former conferences, and he was generally liked. Also, it was plain to see that he had convictions, that he was aggressive, and that he would get things done unhindered by sensitiveness about his color. Any colored leader who can reach that point is likely to find himself in demand by white people who have no idea what the struggle may have cost him. In this way Mr. Harvey is becoming known as a useful interpreter of race questions in white conferences of various types. Not that his speaking is limited to this subject. "For every time that I have spoken about the race question," he says, "I have spoken a dozen times about peace or about some economic question, such as the condition of sharecroppers." For this reason he was delighted to serve on the committee which arranged Toyohiko

Kagawa's seminar on cooperatives in Indianapolis at Christmas time, 1935.

Since 1934 most of the major denominations have organized their own youth fellowships, and thirty-five regional conferences have been held. The first of these was held in Riverside Church, New York City, in March, 1935. Here Mr. Harvey stood up in the nave and reported, as president, what the Christain Youth Council of North America had already done and what it intended to do. Since then he has been in demand as a speaker on the whole program of the Youth Council.

Whatever Mr. Harvey's vocation may be in the future, he is bound to continue working on interracial and interdenominational tasks. His success will depend on his white friends—and they are many—as much as upon himself. There are not a dozen Negro leaders of white Americans in the United States, and so there are few precedents; a pattern for the best way to act will have to be worked out together. The same questions which the Y.M.C.A. secretary raised when Martin Harvey was being considered for the presidency of a junior Y.M.C.A. board will have to be answered all over again by each new group. Where a Negro leader has white friends he is likely to be embarrassed by some of them who make him conspicuous by too much attention, instead of meeting him naturally on the basis of common concern for a task to be done. On the other hand, where he is not known, the Negro leader is sure to find himself in awkward, if not painful, situations. Even the president of the Christian Youth Council, if a Negro, may have to hunt for three hours to find a back-alley restaurant that will serve him. He never knows just what to expect. What is more, he is "always on parade," to use Mr. Harvey's description. He must always make good with no let-up and no exceptions.

Martin Harvey is one of not so many young Negro interpreters. Like the rest, all he asks is to be judged like any other man, and he wants his race judged like any other, on the merits of what it is and does.

II. Juanita E. Jackson

In August, 1934, a thousand young Methodists met at Evanston, Illinois, to form the National Council of Methodist Youth. First they elected their officers. A young Negro woman, Juanita E. Jackson, they chose as their vice president. The officers immediately went into action as a steering committee for the conference. Late one evening the weary commit-

126

tee were ready to eat. "But I can't go with you," their new vice president told them. The others looked at her in amazement, as though they realized for the first time that a Negro girl could not eat at local restaurants with the white delegates to a church conference.

"But you must!" they replied, and "But I can't!" she answered. The indignant group appointed a committee to make a survey of the restaurants near the church to find out which of them would serve the Negro delegates. Of twenty-one restaurants visited, only four proved to be willing, and two of these were small "hamburger" places. The committee reported to the Youth Council, with a recommendation to patronize only these four places. The delegates agreed with enthusiasm, and the result was that the waitresses were swamped. Some of the white delegates volunteered to serve the other customers, and some even went behind the counter to help wash dishes. Friends, they said, can insist on their right to prove that they are friends.

As a result of this experience, the Methodist Youth Council passed a now famous resolution: "We, as Christian youth working together with God for a new world, believe that the present racial discriminations in restaurants, drugstores, and eating-places right at the door of our Council, constitute one of the greatest barriers to the realization of our goal.

"We are convinced that our general objective of Christian brotherhood becomes real only as we face specific situations and live up to that ideal.

"Therefore be it resolved, that the 1012 delegates of the Methodist Youth Council patronize only those establishments which practise no racial discrimination."

Older groups have faced the same difficulty, and there is no question that the Council succeeded in making its point because it found a spirited leader in its new vice president. She knew that the thing ought to be done, and she went ahead with it, putting her natural feelings behind her.

One of the boys on that committee said, "Miss Jackson would be a leader in any group of young people, colored or white."

How did she become that kind of person? Her way to leadership has been swift. Her mother, a former teacher, prepared this child to enter the second grade in Baltimore, Maryland, at the age of four. Juanita was fourteen when she finished high school with honors, after earning her diploma in three years and a half. She went on to Morgan College in Baltimore, a Negro college where there is no competition or pressure from any other race and consequently no barriers for a brilliant and ambitious girl.

Morgan College was founded by the Methodist Episcopal Church in 1867 and is now a state-aided college for Negroes, having won a Class A rating. Its four hundred students come from nineteen states, a fact that broadens the horizon of the local students. Some of the faculty and trustees are colored and some are white, a living demonstration that teamwork can be done.

For two years Miss Jackson maintained an average of A in her studies, and won the Baldwin-Hughes medal for oratory. All this time she was able to work as she pleased without any racial restrictions such as young Negro students suffer on white college campuses. Yet, as she says, "It was freedom, yes, but it was an artificial kind of freedom. It was not natural or right not to be able to know the members of any race but my own."

Presently Miss Jackson transferred to the University of Pennsylvania where she was graduated in 1931 with honors. She found that on this campus a Negro girl could not live in the women's dormitories and could not take part in many of the college activities. At that time, moreover, there was no interracial committee, nor anyone seemingly interested enough to try to change the situation.

After graduation Miss Jackson went back to Baltimore and was soon organizing a group which has since grown into the City-Wide Young People's Forum. A group of young Negroes, many just out of college, with no jobs in sight, began to meet on Friday evenings to discuss the various political, social and economic problems which confronted them, and to try to find out why they could get no jobs and whether anything could be done about the situation. Presently they called in experts from various fields of activity and from the city, state, and federal governments to give them facts. The information was of the kind that leads to action, and Miss Jackson threw herself into finding channels. One was the Interracial Good Will Tours. On the first trip she took a group of twenty white young people with a group of twenty young Negroes to visit Negro churches, hospitals, and business and social organizations, winding up with a banquet and a play at Morgan College. It was all new to the white group, and they insisted on continuing the visits.

Presently the forum began to work toward the employment of Negroes. In Baltimore, as in many cities, chain stores in Negro districts were owned and run by white merchants who refused to employ Negro help, especially in districts where ninety per cent of the customers were Negroes. The forum discussed the situation, decided that it was unfair, cooperated in a Buy Where You Can Work campaign, and after long effort won the point, not with respect to just one store but as a city-wide policy. The forum also led the fight for the appointment of a proportionate number of colored social workers, and secured thousands of signatures to petitions. And here, too, they won. It was through her work in this forum that the National Association for the Advancement of Colored People discovered Miss Jackson. This organization was promoting anti-lynching legislation, and she made an address before the Senate Sub-Committee, which led to her being called later to its staff.

For two summers Miss Jackson was sent traveling and teaching for the Methodist Episcopal Church. In 1933 the Board of Home Missions, through its Bureau of Negro Work, was promoting a series of summer schools for underprivileged Negro ministers. The director took Miss Jackson along with him on a circuit of twelve of these schools to teach a course, "Youth and the Church," to men of her father's age. Most of them had never been able to finish high school and had no idea how to interest the young people of today. Colored young people are as likely to drift to the towns as the whites, but Miss Jackson proceeded to show those faithful rural pastors how to enlist the energies of those who remain at home. She did it with a spirit and vim that caused grateful letters to continue to pour into the office of the Bureau of Negro Work.

In 1934 Miss Jackson went back to the University of Pennsylvania to take her Master's degree in sociology. Before long she was one of the leaders in organizing an interracial commission of the Y.W. C.A. of the university. They made a survey of how Negro students were treated at the university. The commission reported that such students were not welcome in many of the social organizations or in the dormitories. The matter was carried to the president of the university, who ruled that discrimination in the dormitories should cease. So Negro students may now live in the dormitories if they choose to do so.

Miss Jackson made use of these and similar experiences in teaching courses on race relations at white summer conferences. In the summer of 1934 the Methodist Episcopal Church sent her across the country to teach in white institutes. The leader of one institute in California reports that she woke up her students so effectively that many of them have been forming and leading interracial groups ever since. Another white president made a discovery: "Juanita's contribution was made not only in the classroom but wherever she was."

So when Miss Jackson arrived at Evanston in August, 1934, she was already well known. The others quickly recognized her rare gift of dramatization that could make them forget who and where they were, and enter into the experiences of a Negro girl. They went with her in imagination when she had to leave home to take her Master's degree at the University of Pennsylvania because the University of Maryland refused to admit a Negro for graduate study. They could see her being shoved aside on street cars, and being awakened in her berth on a train crossing the Mason and Dixon line, and hurried into the Jim Crow car. "No screens in the windows," she told them, "and smoke and dust and cinders coming in. I sat there from two-thirty in the morning until ten the next morning, fighting back the hatred and anger that involuntarily boiled up, knowing that I had been sent from that other car not because I was less cultured than any of those people in that other car, not because I was less well trained than any of those others, not because I was less of a Christian; but because my skin was brown." [1]

To those who listened the vague idea of race discrimination suddenly ceased to be something they had read about in books and became a matter of rudeness and cruelty to a friend of theirs. Nor did they miss the irony of the situation that their friend had met such experiences while traveling about talking to people of following Christ in everyday life. No wonder that one of the members of that restaurant investigation committee said: "To spend a week with Juanita Jackson is to become a sworn enemy of racial hatred and a life-long advocate of race brotherhood."

In September, 1935, Miss Jackson joined the office staff of the National Association for the Advancement of Colored People in New York City. Now she is a special assistant to the secretary, learning

[1] From *Methodist Youth in Council*, p. 85. National Council of Methodist Youth, Chicago. By permission.

how the organization came to be and what it does, getting ready to travel among its branches in cities and in colleges, developing the youth work of the association. Meanwhile she meets with many groups of young people in churches, on college campuses, in labor groups. Among colored young people she stands for what a Negro girl with a chance for education and training can do and become. Among white young people she shows, to use one of her own phrases, "what we miss when we can't know you, and what you miss when you can't know us."

III. Esther Brown

A certain baseball game was never finished on the grounds of the Bishop Tuttle School in Raleigh, North Carolina. Esther Brown was supposed to be coaching that game, but at the moment she was pinch-hitting for a missing boy. Suddenly a vague message called her indoors, and she flung down the bat and raced off with hair flying. To her dismay, she found herself in the presence of a certain church official who had come from New York City to satisfy himself about her qualifications for a newly created job. Other interviews and correspondence had preceded, and more would follow, but how could Esther Brown know what influence this official's opinion might have?

For one horrible moment she was conscious of her rumpled hair, tennis shoes and gym outfit. Was she about to lose the one opening that had been offered her for work in the Episcopal church? Her graduation from the Bishop Tuttle School was very near, and in that spring of 1931 there were none too many openings for Negro girls. However, her natural balance asserted itself. She forgot her appearance and began to listen eagerly while the visitor outlined what a Negro woman might do for the church as a field worker for the Woman's Auxiliary. Did the visitor decide that a girl who could meet a personal predicament with poise and charm would prove a wise choice? At any rate, his personal comments made to the national headquarters were favorable.

No school guarantees that its graduates will be able to take care of a job that consists largely of predicaments and emergencies. However, Esther Brown had as broad a training as the Episcopal church could at that time provide for a Negro girl. She had graduated from St. Paul's Normal and Industrial School in Lawrenceville, Virginia, and was soon to graduate from the Bishop Tuttle School in Raleigh, North Carolina.

St. Paul's School was founded by one of the first graduates of Hampton Institute, who went on to become the first graduate of the Bishop Payne Divinity School in 1882. Later on, the school came under the American Church Institute for Negroes, but for forty years the founder, who presently became the Venerable James S. Russell, continued to be the principal. He lived to see St. Paul's School give a sound church education to a thousand students a year, for it had become the third largest Negro school in the country and the largest school of the Episcopal church anywhere in the world. When Archdeacon Russell died in 1935, the telegraph company had to put on an additional operator to take care of the flood of telegrams.

Esther Brown grew up on the campus of St. Paul's School, where her father was on the staff. At the time she took for granted certain significant facts about the school. For example, all of the forty-nine buildings had been built by student or graduate labor. That method, she knew, was in the Hampton tradition of self-help. Again the fact that St. Paul's School was a good school stood out in her mind, and not the fact that it was the only colored high school in a fairly large county. Public funds did not provide transportation for colored children, and the day pupils would come walking in, many of them as far as four miles, even through the deep and sticky mud of spring and fall. At present the county matches St. Paul's funds beyond the small tuition fees, but the fact remains that even yet no free high school is provided for Negroes. Meanwhile a constant stream of visitors made St. Paul's School a happy and exciting place to live in.

Among the visitors to the school had been missionaries on furlough from three continents, secretaries from national headquarters of the denomination, and officers of the eight other schools under the American Church Institute for Negroes. Every summer St. Paul's School was the host to a series of church conferences with leadership from outside. In these ways Esther Brown had always been learning what the Episcopal church was doing throughout the world, and she had been getting ready to take her share.

It was some years before she began to wonder why the many white guests never had a meal with the students. She was grown up before she fully realized how hard it is to be a Negro in the United States,

NEGRO LEADERS OF AMERICANS

and by that time she was secure enough in her church life to stand the shock. All this time her life had been so free and happy! She could accomplish whatever she chose with no racial competition or interference, and what she most wanted to do from an early age was church work. At twelve she joined the Episcopal Junior Auxiliary, and remained its president through her high school days. She was also in the cabinet of the Y.W.C.A.

News of the Bishop Tuttle School came to Esther as soon as it was founded in 1925. This school, established by the Woman's Auxiliary and presented to the church, provided at the outset a two-year leadership training course for colored young women in church and community work. A social service center was later built as a laboratory where the students might learn how to carry on many types of Christian work. In addition, local social agencies were (and still are) glad to supervise the work of students from the school. A college degree is now required for admission, but at the time of Esther Brown's entrance, credits from St. Paul's Junior College were accepted.

Between her two years at this school, Miss Brown had a lively experience as a social worker in the summer service for migrant vegetable pickers maintained

as an interdenominational enterprise by the Council
of Women for Home Missions. That summer she
went to Hurlock, Maryland, where a community
center had been established among the colored families who were picking string beans and tomatoes.
"For a while I never wanted to see a tomato again,"
says Miss Brown. Where the crop-tramps come in to
pick one seasonal crop or two, the owner often does
not provide decent living conditions. Life in any of
these centers is a succession of emergencies. The staff
is supposed to include a nurse, a kindergarten teacher,
and a club worker, but any girl may expect to take
her turn anywhere at need. In this case the nurse
arrived late and Miss Brown found herself in sole
charge of six tiny "basket babies," in addition to
cooking the meals and planning the recreation to
keep the children out of the fields. "She is Grade
A," says the national secretary of the Council of
Women for Home Missions.

In 1931 Miss Brown was chosen, as we have seen,
for the job she now holds. The general plan of field
work had already been outlined by the Woman's
Auxiliary in 1922, and several white workers had
already proved that it was true missionary work,
pioneering on a new kind of frontier. Any field

worker goes where she is called anywhere in the United States, and she is not likely to know much about the situation until she arrives. One situation is never like another. She may find herself in a city or in a primitive part of the country without normal companionship, to say nothing of comforts and conveniences. "To do hard things and to do new things: this is what the church demands of its women workers." Thus Professor Adelaide Teague Case of Teachers College has put the blanket orders into one sentence.[1]

Here is Esther Brown, then, arriving in a place where she has probably never been before, in city or country, lonely mission or metropolitan parish. Everywhere there will be new faces, new officers to meet, new situations to learn about, and new emergencies just around the corner. So far Miss Brown is like any field worker. In the nature of the case, however, her appearance at some points creates a new situation calling for special tact. The Woman's Auxiliary may be organized in one of several ways. There may be an organization made up of white women; sometimes there is a parallel Negro organization; and occasionally the members and officers may be of both

[1] From the *Spirit of Missions*, for October, 1935. By permission.

races. So where other field workers have in general one kind of job, Esther Brown may find that she has several.

First of all, like any field worker, Miss Brown listens and learns. The bishop of the diocese in which she is working knows what kind of help the local churches need, and the president of the Woman's Auxiliary knows why she asked for Miss Brown instead of for one of the other field workers. All the leaders of women's work, both white and colored, know how they can use Miss Brown's services while she is there. Evidently there is something here that she can do better than anyone else could do it, and her first job is to find out what it is. First she talks with all those leaders. Then she quietly begins to get acquainted with every group in the parish, men and women, young people and children. She may be visiting from house to house, or at any moment she may be claimed for some special bit of local church work. All this time she is making her survey of the situation, and soon she will be ready to talk it over with the leaders of the Woman's Auxiliary. She will find out what they want to do and will try to help them to do it.

One week Esther Brown may be at a student conference with white or colored Episcopal students where she does work similar to that of a Y.W.C.A. secretary, and organizes the recreation in addition. Immediately afterward she may find herself doing a number of one-night stands in a new region where a general view is the first thing needed. For a month or six weeks after that she may be called to work in a Negro parish, trying to help the women answer the bitter challenge: "Why isn't the church doing more to break down racial barriers?" Her very next call may happen to be to a branch of the Woman's Auxiliary where both white and Negro women are concerned. Here she may settle down to work with them in finding a common task on which they can work together as loyal churchwomen.

Thus her job takes on many forms, but in general it is to help any group, colored or white or both together, to do more effective church work locally, and also to find their share in the worldwide work of the church.

Such a worker has to be always on her tiptoes, alert and sensitive and useful wherever she is. It is a pioneer life. As Esther Brown says: "I have no headquarters except the national office, where I report when my schedule brings me in. I live in two suitcases and a brief case, for I have to be ready to spend a day or a week or a month in the place which has sent for me. I know where I'll be a year from now, but I don't know what I'll be doing till I get there. My job is to study the situation and then get into harness to help do whatever there is to be done."

NINE

HOWARD THURMAN had hardly entered Morehouse
College before he received urgent bids to join every
fraternity on the campus. He turned them all down,
partly because he was working his way through, but
also because he really believed that fraternities are
undemocratic. For a while he went his lonely way,
but he won first rank in his class that year. What was
more surprising, he won it again in his junior and
senior years. In a class of one hundred and fifty, he
was the unanimous choice for the office of sophomore
class president. As a junior he walked away with the
Edgar Allan Poe Short Story Prize and the Cham-
berlain Prize for Scripture Reading. In his senior
year he was elected president of the campus Y.M.
C.A. and president of the Atlanta Student Council,
an interracial body with members from all the colleges in Atlanta, colored and white. His mates had
chosen him as their representative to the national
Y.M.C.A. conference in Cincinnati, Ohio; he had

played the leading parts in "Hamlet" and "Othello"; he had proved himself to be an intercollegiate debater of the first rank; he was the editor-in-chief of the class yearbook; and he became the valedictorian of his class. Howard Thurman needed no fraternity politics to secure honors for him. He had earned the right to say what he pleased and still be popular. Yet all this time this fatherless boy had been working thirty-six hours a week during the college year and through all his vacations, to pay his college expenses.

Ten years previously Howard Thurman had been living in a different world; he was a colored boy in a poor home in Daytona Beach, Florida. A story which he tells about his mother gives the local atmosphere. In 1910 Halley's comet was expected, and this Negro community had been thrown into terror by wild rumors about it. What happened to Howard Thurman is so important that it should be given in his own words.

"When Halley's comet visited our solar system I was a little boy living in a sawmill village in Florida. I had not seen the comet up to the time of my story because my mother made me go to bed with the going down of the sun. I had heard about it.

"I had heard also about a man who had been up

to the sawmill attempting to sell the owner 'comet pills' at so much per box, the theory being that if you took the pills according to directions you would not be consumed when the tail of the comet struck the earth. During the days of the comet it seemed as if the sawmill owner was beginning to treat those who worked for him as if they were human beings.

"One night my mother came to my bed to ask if I wanted to see the giant in the sky. Together we stood underneath the great Florida stars watching the wonderful sight. I shall never forget it if I live forever.

"After a few moments I asked my mother what would happen to us if the comet fell out of the sky. There was silence—I felt her arm tighten around me, and in her face I saw a look that I had seen sometimes before when I came into her room and found her at prayer. 'Nothing,' she said; 'God will take care of you.'

"Her son has not worn blinders through the world since that time. He knows that life is as hard as pig iron, but the deeply lying faith that captured his spirit in that lucid moment has never quite deserted him in all the experiences of life."

How could a boy make his way forward out of

such circumstances as those into which Howard
Thurman was born? Howard's father died early, and
the family had a hard struggle to live. Yet both his
mother and grandmother insisted that Howard must
get an education somehow. "Grandmother held it all
the more compellingly before me," says Mr. Thurman, "because she herself had been born a slave and
could neither read nor write." He finished the grade
school at Daytona Beach, with extra coaching from a
friendly principal during the noon hours. The nearest high school was a Baptist mission school two
hundred miles away.

The first problem was to get a trunk, and the second was to pay the railroad fare of $3.50. The fare
was more than covered by $5.00 which Howard
Thurman managed to scrape together by working
after school hours, and he was given an ancient trunk
without a tray, lock or handles. When he got this
trunk to the station, the baggage man refused to
check it because of its dilapidated condition, and the
express agent demanded $1.80 for shipping it. For-
tunately a Negro man who had overheard the con-
versation saw the boy's dilemma and paid the money.
Howard Thurman arrived at Florida Baptist Academy with one dollar and without a full outfit of

clothes. Some of the students made fun of him, but others sympathized with him and tried to help him because he was in such dead earnest about getting an education.

The tuition in the academy was a dollar and a half a month, and Howard Thurman earned this amount penny by penny, pressing clothes for the townsfolk and doing any odd job he could find. Relatives who had offered him a room in their house lived two miles from school. Daily he walked the four miles, and he was not able to allow himself more than one meal a day during that first year.

During vacation Howard Thurman sold peanuts and shrimps to get the money to go back to school, and he also helped his mother do laundry work so that she could rest while he was at home. The amount he could earn was small, and when he returned to school he was greatly in need of clothes. A well-wisher gave him one dollar to get a pair of pants, but he used it to purchase a book he needed for the next term. During this year he lived in the school and was given a job scrubbing floors, which meant part of his expenses.

At one point in Howard Thurman's junior year he reached a place where he had to have twenty dol-

lars or leave school, and the chance for getting it
seemed as remote as for getting twenty thousand
dollars. He prayed about it, as he did about everything, and the way was unexpectedly opened. A
white man, visiting that mission school, was saying to
the principal at almost that same moment:

"I have educated a Chinese boy. I have educated
a Japanese boy. I have educated a Caucasian and all
of them are making good. I want now to educate a
Negro boy. Choose one for me from among your
students."

"I have the boy," the principal replied instantly.
"His name is Howard Thurman."

"I'll help him forward as far as he is willing to
go," said the white man in conclusion. He lent the
money to cover expenses during Howard Thurman's
senior year, and continued the loans to him at Morehouse College. The whole amount was never more
than a hundred dollars a year, and Howard continued
to do outside work thirty-six hours a week during his
four years of college, but the encouragement and the
friendship that resulted were beyond any money
value.

By this period in his life Howard Thurman knew
that he was going to become a minister. During his

senior year at the Florida Baptist Academy he had
been licensed to preach, and he had continued to
preach while in college as often as his work would
permit and also in his home town during vacations.

But in order to start from the broadest possible
foundation, he majored in economics. "I wanted to
come into the ministry with my eyes wide open to
the way people have to live," he says.

While Howard Thurman was still in the Florida
Baptist Academy, the Y.M.C.A. selected him to go
as its delegate to the conference at King's Mountain,
North Carolina. Here the boy met Max Yergan, back
on furlough from distinguished work as the Negro
Y.M.C.A. secretary for South Africa. That meeting
brought another continent into Howard Thurman's
view for the first time. Here also he met Dr.
Mordecai Johnson, now the president of Howard
University but then the secretary of the conference.
"He had the most powerful intellect of any person
that I had met up to that time," says Mr. Thurman.
After the conference he wrote to Dr. Johnson asking
for advice about his life work and saying that he
wanted to do something hard. "He didn't write down
to the fifteen-year-old boy that I was," Mr. Thurman remembers; "he answered me as man to man."

It was the beginning of a continuing friendship between the two.

Mordecai Johnson had taken his theological training at Rochester Theological Seminary in Rochester, New York, and Howard Thurman made up his mind to go there too. He entered in 1923, after his graduation from Morehouse College. Here the colored students are not made conspicuous by separate registration as is the case in some seminaries. Also, white students treat the two or three Negroes who are living in the dormitories each year as they treat anyone; that is, a man has the chance to make good on his merits. Howard Thurman was popular and carried his work well, also, though he was still earning his way.

In his second year at the seminary, Mr. Thurman met the national director for Y.W.C.A. conferences. He had already been speaking at local gatherings, and this woman convinced him that he should be reaching a larger field. So during his senior year he was sent out as a leader in student conferences throughout New York state. After graduation, while he was pastor of a church in Oberlin, Ohio, the state Y.M.C.A. sent him out on similar work. Through contacts made in this way he was presently called to

take part in the student conference at Lake Geneva,
Wisconsin. More and more he was asked to take
speaking engagements until he has become known
from coast to coast as a leader of high school and
college students, both Negro and white. Students
always seem to recognize him as a man who has won
his own hard fights, and they always connect his vic-
tory with God. As one student writes: "Some men
talk about God, which is of value if it inspires devotion to him. But when Howard Thurman speaks, you
somehow experience God. He seems to take God with
him; or, rather, he seems propelled by God."

After two years in Oberlin, Mr. Thurman was
called back to his own college to teach a course in
philosophy and a course in biblical literature in Spelman, a girls' college on a nearby campus. He was also
religious adviser for the students of both colleges.
Students would seek him out for help on delicate
matters that they would have been afraid to discuss
with any other member of the faculty.

Presently Howard Thurman applied to the National Council on Religion and Higher Education for
a scholarship. This body administers the fund set
aside by Professor Charles Foster Kent of Yale for
helping young people, whether in college or already

starting on their life work, who have proved their ability to see religion in the whole of life. Year by year the colleges of this country are combed for their best students, with no more regard for color of skin than for color of eyes. A year of further study is then made possible. When Mr. Thurman received his award, he made for Haverford College because Rufus Jones was there. Rufus Jones had written *Finding the Trail of Life,* that story of a boy's developing religion which has helped to make religion real to many a boy and girl. "He had what I wanted," says Mr. Thurman; "a combination of insight and social feeling." So Morehouse College granted leave of absence, and Mr. Thurman went off to be made at home in Rufus Jones's classes.

In the following summer the chaplain of Howard University in Washington, D. C., resigned, and Howard Thurman was called to the vacant position. This Negro university, organized by General O. O. Howard in 1867, is supported by government funds, and just before it called Howard Thurman it had received a grant of more than two million dollars for building and maintenance.

When he was offered the position Mr. Thurman protested modestly, "But what could I do?"

Indeed this coeducational city university with two thousand students from all parts of the United States and even from abroad was very different from small church colleges like Spelman and Morehouse in which Mr. Thurman had taught. And he was entirely unconscious of what one of his former professors describes as his "almost titanic power as a preacher," to say nothing of his unusual gifts of sympathy and understanding. Fortunately the president of Howard University, Dr. Mordecai Johnson, had known Mr. Thurman for twelve years and overrode all his objections.

"Your job during our school year," said Dr. Johnson, "will be to do whatever you want to do. In the summers you'll be as free as ever for your leadership in student conferences."

And that decision was fortunate for all concerned, because any student conference that has had Mr. Thurman once is likely to demand his return. He has gone year after year to Asilomar, the famous conference center in California, as a leader for men and women, for high school students, and for business girls. He has never been asked to come as a resource person on race relations, but always as a religious leader. Student after student has said:

155

"Knowing Howard Thurman has changed my whole attitude toward Negroes. I think of them as individuals now, and not as a race."

On one of these annual trips to the Pacific coast, Mr. Thurman was invited to meet some university students informally at tea in a Palo Alto home. A Southern girl went reluctantly, unwilling to meet a Negro guest on equal terms, and prepared to leave if he started "lecturing about the race problem." He did nothing of the sort; he began to share what he knows about God. As he talked, the Southern girl's reluctance melted away. Afterward, she wrote:

He sat—
His black, black face
Fading into the shadows of the room,
We sat—
The white masks of our faces
Trying to hide our thoughts
As his quiet voice
Spoke simply—humbly—of a Lord he had found.

And when he was done
We all sat—
Each measuring his standards against our own.
There was pure silence in that room.

We were so far below—
Behind—that man who humbly sat before his Maker.
And we are tempted to scorn his race!
God has such simple ways of showing us our wrong
If we but sit at times—and listen.[1]

Not a word had been said about race relations, and yet certain avenues, closed for years, had been opened for traffic in this girl's mind. She saw the heights on which Mr. Thurman lived, and dimly felt the struggle that had been necessary to reach them.

As for the job at Howard University, a friend gives this very informal description. "Oh, yes, Howard does teach a course or two in the school of religion. He's supposed to teach systematic theology among other things, and I suppose he does take his class through the growth of certain ideas in the development of the Christian church. But that's the least thing he does. After the class session he goes home —he has a house on the campus—and the students, boys and girls both, tread a path to his door at all hours of the day and night."

It is well to show Mr. Thurman surrounded by students who need him, but the dean of the school

[1] By Marion Burke Pratt, Menlo Park, California.

of religion and the president of the university have something more definite to say about the job. Mr. Thurman is an associate professor in the school of religion, in which he teaches several courses. He is also chairman of the university's committee on religious life, which selects the speakers for the Sunday religious services. In this capacity he has built up a Sunday service at Howard University that ranks high among college services throughout the country. In addition, he is still constantly sought for student conferences. With all this he loves to spend as much time as possible in his home with his family.

A recent close-up view of Mr. Thurman and his wife in a summer conference comes from a white leader at the Y.W.C.A. Conference of New England Colleges, held annually in the Maqua region in Maine. "Together they were the focus around which that conference turned," she writes. "Mrs. Thurman is a trained musician with a degree from a conservatory of music. Under her leadership singing became not another way of taking up time in a worship service but the pouring forth of souls in joy and thoughtfulness. The girls trusted her knowledge of the spirit and of the music to give them the deepest understanding of the possibilities of some familiar hymn. Her way of playing the piano was a revelation of the power of music in worship. Howard's worship services were revelations, too, of the power of silence and of beauty in worship, of the beauty of simplicity. Of course the experience of these college girls was limited, and they could not follow all that Howard had found out about God, but *they knew that he knew*."

In 1935 the Student Christian Movement of India, Burma, and Ceylon sent a unique request to the leaders of the student movement in this country. They asked that a delegation of American Negroes be sent to talk with their students. This was the first time such a thing had ever happened. The four Negroes selected for this Friendship Delegation, as it was called, were Mr. Thurman and Mrs. Thurman, and the Rev. Edgar G. Carroll and Mrs. Carroll. They sailed in September, 1935, and returned in April, 1936. Between October and March they visited fifty-three college and university centers, traveling from Ceylon to Peshawar on the northwest frontier of India, and from Rangoon, Burma, to Bombay. At every point their student hosts had arranged for them to see examples of Indian music, architecture, painting, dances, arts and crafts. At every point, too, there was an avalanche of keen and penetrating questions which stretched one-hour appointments into three and four hours. The questions were exceedingly hard to answer. "I find at every point," wrote Mr. Thurman, "that I am using whatever is mine as a result of a lifetime of thought and study. No harder job will ever be mine in this world."

These are only two of the questions that Mr. Thurman and his friends met at every turn: "Does it make any difference in race feeling on the part of white Americans when Negroes become Christians? Do you have caste distinctions in the Christian church in America?"

TEN

HER UNFINISHED TASK

JULIETTE DERRICOTTE is speaking. "It's not just my own story, it might be anybody's story, the story of hundreds of people. I was born in a little town down South where I never talked with a white person naturally until I went to college. My mother was a seamstress who worked mostly for white people. She would not expose us to humiliation—there were nine of us children—and so she never sent us to white homes with work she had finished."

Her mother was a seamstress and her father was a cobbler. Juliette grew up to be such a girl that in college no occasion was complete without her. Within five years after her graduation thousands of college students across this country knew and loved her. Ten years after graduation, students in Europe, India, China and Japan had come to know and love her too, because she, an American Negro, understood their struggles to win their freedom. In 1928 she told her story to a friend who is glad to reproduce it here.

Juliette's home in Athens, Georgia, was one of the better colored homes and her parents were wiser than most. They brought up their children in the strictest religious tradition, and yet they knew how to temper it with gentleness. Because they were a colored family in a Georgia town, the children learned very early that certain things were different for them. They came to know, for instance, that in any store they would be the last to be waited on. They accepted the fact, but they didn't talk about it.

Juliette went through the public schools of Athens with a deep longing for education, never dreaming that it could be managed. However, a student re-cruiting agent convinced her mother that this daugh-ter should go off to Talladega College in Talladega, Alabama. It was then a tiny school and college under the American Missionary Association. Thrifty parents could just manage the expenses where tuition was $2.50 a month, and board and room was $12.50 a month—a college education for $150 a year! Juli-ette's mother had a special reason for sending her to this school where all the professors were white men and women. She believed that her daughter would be better prepared for life in a white man's world if she met it on friendly terms in a missionary college.

Juliette, though, took a whole year to get used to it. Some of the students had taken the next train home when they found that all the professors were white. Juliette stood her ground, but it was a long year's struggle. Fortunately her ability was soon discovered.

"I shall never forget one professor," said Miss Derricotte ten years later, "who sought me out to tell me that he thought I ought to try for a public speaking prize that gave tuition. 'Of course I can't do it,' I said, but he was so sure I could that he found a coach to help me, and I won! That gave me my first confidence in myself." [1]

After that experience Juliette was not long in finding herself. Even in that first year all her grades were over ninety, and she kept that average all the way through. She was not brilliant, but she was the slow and glowing kind of student. At the same time she went in for all kinds of activities. A classmate afterward remarked, "One could hardly have imagined a college function without Jule." She was on the intercollegiate debating team, she was twice chosen as president of the Y.W.C.A., and she helped to plan the stunts and games for the joint parties and

[1] From "I Am Myself," as told to Mary Jenness. By permission of the American Missionary Association.

163

the Saturday hikes. As in other Negro colleges at that period, student strikes were frequent. Juliette usually became the spokesman for the faculty, braving the charge of being "faculty pet," and yet remained popular with the students. On one occasion, and that the most serious, she decided that the students were right in their demands, took a strong stand with them, and helped them win. In her junior year she was appointed as assistant to the matron of Foy Cottage, where the college girls lived. The matron was Scotch and stern, the girls were lively, and Juliette as full of fun as any of them. Yet she gained and kept the good will of both sides, always able to interpret one to the other. No wonder that, twelve years later, she became the only woman trustee of Talladega College.

That student recruiting agent had continued to be Juliette's adviser and friend. He had watched her remarkable influence in the Y.W.C.A., and in her junior year he suggested that she should try for Y.W.C.A. work after graduation. At that time teaching was the only door wide open to a Negro woman, and his suggestion seemed almost impossible; yet Juliette liked it. She took the first chance to talk it over with a Y.W.C.A. field secretary. "She showed me," said Miss Derricotte, "that if I really wanted it hard enough, I could do that—or anything else. So when I graduated in 1918, I went North immediately and took the summer course at the National Y.W.C.A. Training School in New York City. I worked, how I worked! In the fall, I was made traveling secretary for some of the colleges where there were colored students not allowed in the white Christian associations.

"That year was the most miserable year of my life! I was unhappy in the office, where I went to my desk alone, ate alone, and left the building alone. All this time I was so puzzled to hear people talking of Christian brotherhood! But the worst thing was that I did not feel that I was getting anywhere with my job. Once a year I would go to a college where there were colored girls, help them to organize their cabinet, and set them going until I could come around again. But all the time, though I suppose we were developing their initiative, we were keeping them just as separate as ever. We hadn't begun to attack the problem of interracial relations."

All this was before Juliette Derricotte grew out of thinking of herself as a Negro secretary and began to realize that she was a student secretary. When she did realize it, in a way that will be told presently, she began to do pioneer work which made the student Christian associations the interracial fellowship that they are now. The things that she was the first to plan, such as student forums for colored and white girls, and interracial week-end conferences, have been built into the whole plan and program of the National Student Council.

Here is Juliette Derricotte's own story of how she stopped being a colored girl and became an interpreter. "Five years ago something happened that made my whole life over, and I've been a different person ever since. A Western woman told us how bitter the feeling was between white and colored students in some of the Mid-West universities. From the South there had been a large influx of white students and also of Negroes; and they simply did not know how to get on together when they met in Kansas or Missouri or Oklahoma. It just happened that I was the person who was free to go out to see what ought to be done. A white secretary went with me. I didn't know her, though we had been working in the same building, but we liked each other as soon as we got acquainted on this trip.

"When we got to our university, the colored girls

wouldn't talk to me when Miss —— was around. And the white girls wouldn't talk to her when I was there. So we talked with them in separate corners till we understood. Then we chose ten white girls and ten Negro girls and brought them together to work this thing out.

" 'How can you call yourselves Christians?' we asked. 'How can you say that you want to bring freedom to all people when there are on your own campus people that you won't speak to?' We made them face it, first the white Y.W.C.A. girls, and then both together. They did. After we left they wanted to go on, and we gave them a simple outline of some questions that neither group had thought about before. For example, How did the Negro get here in the United States? What has slavery done for him, and for the white people? (That was hard for both of them.) What contribution has the Negro made in art, in music, in religion? Is it possible that he has something that the white man needs for complete living?

"Our group worked hard on these questions for a year. All that time I kept answering their letters about it. The next year, they had learned so much together that they went out to teach their university. Programs of Negro music or Negro poetry were put on. Bars were taken down. Colored girls were sought out and invited to the Y.W.C.A., welcomed when they got there, and urged to work on committees. The next year, the whole Y.W.C.A. dropped the interracial issue and together, white and colored, went out to clean up on that campus the things that were not Christian! So I learned that the most worth while thing to do is to be yourself and do your own work, not to attack just the interracial question."

In discovering what these students could do together Juliette Derricotte had begun to discover herself. From this time on she came to work easily with students of any race. Part of her job was still the planning of student conferences in colored colleges. One friend pictures such a conference in a tiny college in Mississippi, seven miles from a half-dead town. Here the men and women, nearly all of them working their way, would invite thirty or forty colored students from other colleges south to New Orleans and north to Tennessee. Everyone was poor but could manage fifty cents for registration and the dollar guest fee for a week-end conference. To these isolated students, most of them off the farm, Miss Derricotte would bring the best ideas she had to offer out of her experience and wide contacts, and the best college leadership that she could command. She herself would come, radiant and sure, fairly breathing confidence into some of those shy, awkward students whose morale had collapsed because they felt themselves already beaten in a struggle too great for them. They would remember her all their lives as one who had put new heart into them.

More and more Miss Derricotte came to be in demand in white colleges and at white conferences. For example, she was often called to the famous conference grounds at Asilomar, California. On the first occasion, "I went not to represent Negroes," she said, "but to take a series of ten worship services. At my first service, there was a white woman who had just refused to take a Negro girl in her car from the station to the conference. At the close of the service she said to her friend, 'Wasn't that wonderful?' 'Yes,' said her friend, 'that is one of the finest colored girls I know.' 'Was she *a colored girl?*' asked the scandalized woman. That evening this woman sat opposite me at a picnic and never once spoke to me. But the day the conference closed, she came to me with tears in her eyes. 'My dear,' she said, 'I want you to know that you have opened a whole new world to me.' It was all because I had just been myself. Most of the time I never realize that I am a Negro at all, though in some groups I have to think of it, at least at the start."

For eleven years Miss Derricotte traveled across the country, and many colleges and conferences came to know her well. Such experiences as the one described above kept coming to her over and over again in each new white group, and it could never have been easy to meet them. How did she learn to go on without bitterness? A Y.M.C.A. secretary of the same period says it was partly because she learned to forget herself in the larger task of making people understand each other. "She was able to work as a practitioner," he says, "to get down to the roots and work from there. At the same time she had a rare forward thrust like a prophet, toward the next thing that had to be done. Then, too, she had a spirit of play that would often cause a hostile group to melt in laughter."

Take a certain occasion. "An interracial meeting began on a hot July evening that wilted everybody down to a sort of dutiful doggedness by nine o'clock. Hence the last speaker was welcomed with mixed emotions—till one actually saw her. A slender lovely girl in white arose, threw back her head and laughed.

She wore a white crepe dress, embroidered in yellow patterns that spilled from her shoulders down to her knees, as though she stood behind a clump of forsythia, parting the branches to laugh through. And such a laugh! A golden tone, a happy understanding sound that embraced all those tired uncomfortable people and raised them to a higher level. Everybody cheered up and listened

"This is the kind of thing they heard. 'You can't know what it does to a girl, inside of her, when she sits down at the table in a college cafeteria and another girl rises after one look and takes her food to another table.' A little shudder ran through the audience; a girl like this, to be reporting a thing like that! Yet the wonder was, as they thought it over, that a girl like this had become capable of living through and around and above 'a thing like that.' " [1]

In 1924 Juliette Derricotte was sent to England to represent American college students at the session of the general committee of the World's Student Christian Federation, meeting at High Leigh. This general committee is an elected group of representatives from forty-five student Christian movements

[1] Memorial Number for Juliette Derricotte of the *Interracial News Bulletin*, Student Council of the Y.W.C.A., March, 1932. By permission.

of the world who meet every two years to discuss what Christian students in a world like ours ought to do. When she sailed Miss Derricotte found that in the liner's dining room persons of a darker color were deftly steered to tables at the side. However, she had long since ceased to be troubled by incidents of that sort. At High Leigh she proved to be a revelation to students, both European and Oriental, who had never before seen an American Negro. Some of them took her for an American Indian and wondered if she would wear her "native costume" as several of the other girls did. The ones who had been most puzzled at the beginning became her firmest friends before the close of the conference.

Once again Juliette Derricotte was chosen as a delegate to the World's Student Christian Federation, and this time, in 1928, the meetings were to be held on one of the estates of the Maharajah of Mysore, in India. Just before she sailed she had been working on a book of worship services for students, using the materials of all lands and of all ages, and doing it with delight, not as a colored secretary but as herself. The work was good preparation for a trip where, as one of her companions said, "She was by all odds the most understanding and the most useful person in our group. She was speaking for American womanhood and for the whole student movement."

So she spoke to Indian girls of the Christian College in Madras, who had always seen their mothers walk five paces behind their fathers on the street. She knew how to speak not for Negro girls alone but for all women underprivileged in the modern world. "We are not fighting for our rights," she said, "but we are fighting for our right to contribute what we have to give." The Indian university students in return bombarded her with questions about the American Negro. "Do you dress like other Americans?" they demanded. "Do you feel loyal to a government that oppresses you? Are you as prejudiced against white people as we are? Do you think that race prejudice is born in people, or is it taught? Why do our students have to wear turbans when they go to your country, to avoid being treated like American Negroes?"

As for the conference, the most important part of it seemed to be what the ninety student delegates from four continents were telling each other on the side. Miss Derricotte's Korean tent-mate kept her awake until two in the morning telling her that even as an American Negro she could know nothing of race prejudice, segregation and discrimination; that to know the real meaning of these words she would have to be a Korean living under the rule of a foreign government. The next day a Japanese girl begged her to tell why the United States government discriminated against the Japanese in the immigration ruling of 1924. Everywhere on the grounds the white delegates from South Africa were telling what a real spiritual experience they had had when they could shake hands with Max Yergan, the Negro Y.M.C.A. secretary for South Africa. They were glad to have a chance to know him at last and plan with him as they could never do at home. An Indian girl welcomed the chance to tell a British woman how she had been kept standing, waiting for a seat in church until all the whites were seated, and one Britisher came to understand how another woman felt about something that she herself had taken for granted. The meeting itself, as Miss Derricotte said afterward, was a prophecy of what might happen to all the world. With all the bitterness and prejudice there might be between any two countries or within any one of them, still these ninety students were able to meet here as friends, and work and play and plan together.

For seven weeks Juliette Derricotte stayed in
India. From the Maharajah's furnished camp in
Mysore she went on to live in Y.W.C.A.'s with
Anglo-Indians; in an Indian student hostel; in a
deserted military camp with five hundred students
from India, Burma, and Ceylon; in mission schools;
in Indian homes; and in European hotels. In these
ways she saw so much more of India than most trav-
elers do that she was never able to forget the experience. Following this conference she went on to China
and Japan and in brief meetings tried to help the students of those countries to understand themselves.
She returned to tell American students of all races
that the young men and women of the whole world
are struggling with the same problems. She never
got away from the memories of India. Later she
wrote: "I don't know how to answer my friends who
say, 'Did you have a wonderful time?' Of course it
was most interesting, but how can I say that I am no
longer free; that the wealth as well as the poverty
of India haunts me; that I ache with actual physical
pain when I remember the struggles of all India today, religious, caste, economic, social, political? How
can I tell of the control which oil and rubber and
jute have in the relation to East and West, or ex-

plain how back of oil and rubber and jute are the more fundamental and eternal puzzles of economics, race, and religion? My head whirls. . . ."[1]

With all these questions unanswered, Juliette Derricotte began to feel the need of settling down in one spot to work more permanently with one group of students. So in 1929 she resigned from her job as the National Student Secretary for the Y.W.C.A. and became the dean of women at Fisk University. Here was a red-hot center of student problems. The school had grown and changed beyond belief since it was opened in discarded hospital barracks in 1865. Now it includes a coeducational college of liberal arts, as well as a graduate school, including thousands of students, men and women. Here, just as at Talladega College in the early days, the regulations for women students were strict and old fashioned, far behind the regulations for men, and childish in comparison with those familiar to white college students. There was a student government organization for women, but in the past it had been under faculty control. Miss Derricotte proceeded to think out a program. It included a new building for freshman

[1] From "The Student Conference at Mysore, India," by Juliette Derricotte, *The Crisis*, August, 1929. By permission.

women; also an organization that would help the students to find out what work they could do after graduation. The student government must be made over into a growing concern, with the hands of the faculty kept strictly off. In a personal letter she wrote:

"I want a group of senior women who are to be left absolutely on their own, subject only to the regulations a girl makes for herself, the college stepping in only at the request of the girl or when she persists in being very indiscreet. I feel very strongly that our senior women, though very much freer than practically all of the other Negro college women students, are so childish and irresponsible that unless we free them and put them on their own, we simply prolong their adjustment to life situations."

Results were very slow in coming in so disturbed a center, but at least the students came to trust Miss Derricotte. She began by living outside of the girls' dormitory, where formerly the deans had always been expected to act as police women, and retreated to a cottage where she could be sought out as a friend. At first the students could not understand their new dean. What, freedom of action to be allowed? That was an amazing idea. The student was to be respon-

sible to herself for what she did with her freedom?
That idea was astounding. The leaven of it was just
beginning to work when the tragedy happened that
sent a chill of horror through Miss Derricotte's
friends around the world. She was killed in an auto-
mobile accident in November, 1931.

During all these years Juliette Derricotte had been
a bulwark for her family, sending a younger sister
through college, helping to pay off the mortgage on
the home, and always ready with counsel and companionship. Now she was planning to go home for
Thanksgiving on a matter of family business. She
drove her own car in order to escape the limitations
of Jim Crow trains, taking with her three students
whose homes were in Georgia. Just outside the town
of Dalton, Georgia, her car collided with one driven
by a white man. It was overturned, the students were
thrown out, and she and one of the girls were seriously injured. The town of Dalton has a hospital for
whites, but the hospital has never had a Negro ward.
The two injured colored women were treated by two
local white doctors in their offices and were then re-
moved to the cottage of an untrained Negro woman
who was a "practical nurse." This cottage was the
only place in Dalton where ill or injured Negroes

might be cared for. Some time later, against the advice of the white doctor, the two colored women were moved in an ambulance over the rough road to Chattanooga, Tennessee, where there is a small hospital for Negroes. The injured student died on the way, and Miss Derricotte died twenty-six hours after the accident.

The story is told in detail in a special report made by the Commission on Interracial Cooperation and in Marion Cuthbert's book, *Juliette Derricotte*. What happened would have had to happen to any seriously injured Negro. Proper treatment and care could have been given in the white hospital, but no one even thought of taking them there because they were colored. Such was the fixed and unyielding pattern of the community.

After the blinding shock of her death, thoughtful people came to see why that social pattern is wrong. It is wrong precisely because it is too rigid to recognize that color has nothing to do with the value of human life. Miss Derricotte emphasized by her death what she had always said with her life.

Memorial services were held all over the country. Howard Thurman, a friend of long standing, conducted the one held in Athens, Georgia. "There is work to be done," he said, "and ghosts will drive us on; this is an unfinished world; she leaves an unfinished task. Who shall take it up? Driven by the power of her spirit we dedicate ourselves anew to the process within this imperfect world." [1]

Juliette Derricotte never once thought that her job was done when she had secured the facts. She wanted to know why they were so, what the causes were, and what the results. She wanted to know how people felt about the facts, and how that feeling could be changed. Only then she could go ahead in a spirit of confidence and of gaiety and of beauty, often saying, "There is so much more to know than I am accustomed to knowing, and so much more to love than I am accustomed to loving." Somewhere ahead, she thought, "all may be one." That is the spirit in which her countless friends are going ahead with her unfinished task.

[1] From *The Crisis*, March, 1932. By permission.